Flourishing in the First Five Years

Connecting Implications from Mind, Brain, and Education Research to the Development of Young Children

Donna Wilson and Marcus Conyers

ROWMAN & LITTLEFIELD EDUCATION
A division of
ROWMAN & LITTLEFIELD
Lanham • Boulder • New York • Toronto • Plymouth, UK

Published by Rowman & Littlefield Education
A division of Rowman & Littlefield
4501 Forbes Boulevard, Suite 200, Lanham, Maryland 20706
www.rowman.com

10 Thornbury Road, Plymouth PL6 7PP, United Kingdom

British Library Cataloguing in Publication Information Available

Library of Congress Cataloging-in-Publication Data

Wilson, Donna (Donna Lee)
Flourishing in the first five years : connecting implications from mind, brain, and education research
to the development of young children / Donna Wilson and Marcus Conyers.
pages cm
Includes bibliographical references and index.
ISBN 978-1-4758-0317-4 (cloth : alk. paper)—ISBN 978-1-4758-0318-1 (pbk. : alk. paper)—ISBN
978-1-4758-0319-8 (electronic : alk. paper)
1. Learning, Psychology of. 2. Learning—Physiological aspects. 3. Brain. I. Conyers, Marcus. II.
Title.
LB1060.W5527 2013
370.15'23—dc23
2013026991

∞™ The paper used in this publication meets the minimum requirements of American
National Standard for Information Sciences Permanence of Paper for Printed Library
Materials, ANSI/NISO Z39.48-1992.

Printed in the United States of America

Contents

Preface

As busy as young children always seem to be, their minds are even busier. Every experience they have is a learning experience, forging and reinforcing connections among brain cells and laying the foundation for their formal education. This text for early childhood educators, caregivers, and parents of infants, toddlers, and preschoolers introduces relevant findings from mind, brain, and education research and examines the practical implications of those findings for the lives of young children.

Our vision for this book, as promised in its title, is to help every child flourish in his or her early years and be ready to thrive on the first day of school—and every day thereafter.

Toward that end, we explore

- how and why early childhood educators, caregivers, and parents can become "caring coaches" to help young children develop self-control, critical thinking, and problem-solving abilities;
- how learning changes the brain and what that means for every child to be able to achieve his or her unique potential;
- how to encourage young children to become "the boss of their brains" by developing self-control and learning age-appropriate critical-thinking skills;
- what discoveries about learning through imitation and mirror neurons mean for early childhood educators, parents, and other caring adults in children's lives;
- how to optimize the AEIOU learning cycle that recurs daily at home and in the early childhood center;
- what neuroscientists have learned about the developing brains of infants and young children;
- why modeling and reinforcing an optimistic outlook may improve learning outcomes;
- how to support the development of early literacy, problem-solving, and creative abilities;

- what roles healthy nutrition and regular physical activity play in supporting learning; and
- how to identify and address risks to healthy development.

CONTENT OVERVIEW

The concepts referenced above are organized into seven chapters that, taken collectively, give early childhood educators, parents, and other caregivers important insights into children during their first five years of development.

Chapter 1 introduces important concepts from the emerging field of educational neuroscience about how young children learn: that the brain changes in response to new experiences, that infants learn naturally through imitation, and that outdated notions about fixed intelligence need to be set aside in favor of an understanding that we all have the capacity to become functionally smarter.

Chapter 2 rounds out this research review with a memorable "by-the-numbers" tour of discoveries about the brain, mind, and child development in recent decades—for example, about how the mind and brain learn, how senses function as the gateway to learning, how we can shape our emotional responses, how children exhibit many forms of intelligence, and how extensive human brain capacity really is.

Chapter 3 explores how the brain and body work together to support cognitive development, underscoring the importance of healthy nutrition, regular physical activity, and adequate sleep. We also discuss how movement and music can help young children attend to learning tasks and enhance their memory of what they have learned.

The power of positivity in support of learning is the topic of Chapter 4. Here we explore the growing body of research about how children who believe that they can achieve what they aim to do are more likely to do so and how educators and parents can model and help instill an optimistic outlook in young children.

Chapter 5 explores recent research about language and early literacy development. It celebrates the power of simple conversations with young children, of playing with language, and of reading, reading, and more reading.

A creative approach to guiding children to develop their problem-solving abilities and learn self-control is presented in Chapter 6. By beginning to learn how to regulate their behaviors and thinking, young children are on the path to becoming the boss of their brains.

Chapter 7 examines risk factors to healthy child development, from prenatal exposure to alcohol and tobacco to the adverse impact of toxic stress, poverty, and child abuse and neglect. By providing this content, we hope to equip early childhood educators with valuable information for parent education and interactions with families and community leaders to encourage involvement in and support for children's learning—one more step toward our goal of helping all children thrive.

We wrap up the central points of the text in our conclusion, and the glossary is designed as a useful reference to key terms introduced throughout this book.

PRACTICAL APPLICATIONS

Several special features are presented to highlight key content and apply the research discussed in these pages.

- **Learning How to Learn** features examples of cognitive assets, or thinking skills, that you can teach and that young children can learn and incorporate into their play and interactions with others.
- **Learn With Us** is a series of "learning stories" that accompany the discussion of cognitive assets. Featuring engaging animal characters, each story includes key terms to introduce to children before sharing the story and follow-up activities to give them the opportunity to practice these cognitive skills.
- **AEIOU in Action** offers examples of a five-step learning cycle (tied to the letters *a*, *e*, *i*, *o*, and *u*) especially suited for early childhood education programs.
- **Engaging With Educators** is a collection of short features in which early childhood educators who earned their graduate degree through the brain-based teaching program we codeveloped with Nova Southeastern University share their perspectives on the principles explored in the text as well as stories from their classrooms.
- **Practical Tips for Early Childhood Educators** is a section at the end of each chapter that features ideas for applying the research and information presented there.

In our work in teacher education, we find that educators are often energized as they learn about recent research that forms the basis for "the science of learning"—and the "art" of their work. Many tell us they are thrilled to find support in this research for teaching approaches they have already found to be effective in their practice. Many of the research findings and applications presented in this text apply to adults as well, so we're pleased to have you join us on this lifelong journey of discovering how the mind learns best!

Introduction

We are setting our sights high in this text, with the aim of sharing with early childhood educators, parents, and other caregivers what mind, brain, and education research has to say about how all children can flourish in their first five years. Another way to look at this core purpose is that we are just practicing one aspect of what we hope to convey here: Owing to brain plasticity and malleable intelligence, nearly all children—and adults as well—have the potential to learn, grow, and thrive.

The primary definitions of the word **flourish** (from *Merriam-Webster's Collegiate Dictionary*, 11th edition) underscore our envisioned outcome for optimizing the learning potential of young children:

1. to grow luxuriantly: *thrive*
2a. to achieve success: *prosper*

There is a great deal of support in exciting research from recent decades about the learning capacity of infants and young children from their earliest days of life and onward. We now know that infants' brains are primed for learning through imitation, as demonstrated by their ability to mimic facial movements (like sticking out one's tongue) just hours after birth. We know that learning changes the function and structure of the brain. We know that this **neuroplasticity** supports the view that intelligence can be enhanced, that it is not fixed at birth (Wilson & Conyers, 2013). And we know that even young children benefit from explicit instruction on how to use a variety of cognitive skills and strategies to support learning.

In our work with tens of thousands of educators in the United States and around the world, it is always exhilarating to see the excitement on participants' faces as we share with them new understandings about the brain's awesome potential to be transformed by experience. To know that the learning experiences orchestrated for young children may positively impact their lives can provide a tremendous boost to the motivation and passion of early childhood educators, parents, and caregivers as they help children make the most of their learning potential.

In particular, when we emphasize the importance of teaching children how to be "the boss of their brains" and develop self-control and cognitive skills, we see metaphorical lightbulbs pop on above their heads as teachers and administrators smile and nod in agreement (Wilson & Conyers, 2011b). And that reaction is even greater when we pass along research findings that indicate the acquisition of these very learnable skills in students' younger years are more predictive of them completing college than are their SAT and ACT scores (Tough, 2012). In the studies in brain-based teaching we codeveloped with Nova Southeastern University as part of a graduate program there, many early childhood educators have taken these lessons to heart—and put them to practice—as they use them to shape their interactions with their young students. The graduate program reflects "the goal of brain-based education . . . to translate brain research into the optimization of the school learning environment" (Miller & DeFina, 2010, p. 142). At the early childhood level, this optimization takes the form of focusing "on the nature and quality of preschool interventions" with the aim "to maximize both student affective gains and academic achievement" (Tayler, 2013, p. 26).

HOW "CARING COACHES" CAN HELP
YOUNG CHILDREN FLOURISH

The relationship that infants and toddlers have with the "caring learning coaches," or facilitators of early learning, in their lives—parents, grandparents, older siblings, caregivers, and early childhood educators—can put them on the best path for flourishing and getting ready to "do school." Young children learn a great deal through playful learning, observation, and exploration of their world, but they also learn in and through their interactions with others. As you guide infants and young children to develop their motor, language, social, and thinking (cognitive) skills, consider four aspects of these interactions that may help optimize how they learn (Wilson & Conyers, 2011b):

1. **Caring**. Young children need to know that the adults on whom they rely care about them and want them to do well. When they feel safe, secure, and cared for, children can then turn their attention to exploring, observing, and trying new things. And when confronted with challenges, children will be more likely to dedicate the persistent effort needed to achieve mastery with your sup-

port and encouragement. Put simply, children will care more about learning when they know you care.

2. **Clear intent**. Before you can accomplish a goal, you need to be able to identify what that goal is and how you can achieve it. Developing your clear intent to help young children flourish involves understanding (a) how they learn, (b) what abilities they can and should develop as toddlers and preschoolers so they are school-ready, and (c) how you can best guide them to develop those abilities. We hope reading this book will help you realize these intentions!

3. **Making meaning**. There are many reasons why children ask "Why?" Perhaps the most fundamental is their desire to understand their surroundings and to relate these new understandings to their growing knowledge base. By viewing every "Why?" (or at least as many of them as you can!) as opportunities to explore and learn *with* children, you can nurture the curious spirit that will facilitate lifelong learning. Asking guiding questions and making suggestions instead of simply supplying answers allows young children to take charge of the learning experience and sets them on a path to become self-directed learners who will thrive in school and beyond.

4. **Transfer**. Learning is an incremental process of amassing knowledge, applying knowledge, and building on existing knowledge. Look for opportunities for children to transfer what they have learned into their everyday lives. As just one example, learning the letters in their picture books can help them see how the act of reading is a necessary part of life—in navigating traffic signs, in choosing ingredients for a recipe at the grocery store, and in planning a fun vacation online. By labeling and modeling how you use the skills young children are just beginning to develop and by recognizing how they are transferring their budding knowledge, you emphasize the value of learning.

Throughout this text, we will continue to explore these and other aspects of how you can guide, support, and encourage young children to make the most of their learning potential in your roles as a caring coach and "lead learner" who demonstrates and shares your own love of discovering new things.

GOOD NEWS FOR LEARNERS OF ALL AGES

There are many good books on early childhood development. This text focuses on the core concepts that we have found generate the most enthusiasm and engagement among early childhood educators and that have a firm foundation in neuroscientific, cognitive, and educational research. The findings and practical implications presented here move beyond more traditional approaches to focus on guiding children to develop an optimistic, can-do approach to learning supported by their familiarity with using the thinking skills we call **cognitive assets** that will serve them well in their futures in school, in the workplace, and in their personal pursuits. These early years are an optimal time to guide children to develop these outlooks and skills; as Tayler (2013) notes, "early parenting practices and preschool preparation, as well as the process of transitioning into school, have been shown to have long-term positive influences on children's cognitive and social development" (p. 25).

We hope you enjoy this text and find the research and applications presented here as exciting as we do. Many teachers who have studied with the graduate program with a major in brain-based teaching tell us they are energized and inspired as they consider the implications of this wide-ranging research—on neuroplasticity, malleable intelligence, learning potential, the Body-Brain System, and the benefits of explicit instruction on the use of cognitive assets. They see applications for their students, their own children, and even themselves in their own learning and professional practice. That brings us to one final crucial point: These discoveries about brain plasticity, intelligence, and learning potential apply not just to young children but to older children, adolescents, teenagers, and adults of all ages. We all have the capacity to be lifelong learners. That means it is never too early—or too late—to dream a dream and pursue it.

We are not alone in our belief that the world would be a better, happier place if everyone understood that they have the capacity to learn, to grow, to become better at the skills they need to realize their goals. In his book *Flourish*, Martin Seligman (2011) defines well-being as the state to which we all aspire and describes the elements of well-being as positive emotion, engagement in endeavors we enjoy and find fulfilling and in which we find meaning, positive relationships, and feelings of accomplishment. Seligman calls for "a new prosperity, one that takes flourishing seriously as the goal of education and of parenting" (p. 97). We strongly concur and share a vision that we can set young children on a path to well-being by

- fostering a caring, positive learning environment with many opportunities for playful learning and exploration,
- guiding them to develop cognitive and self-regulatory skills that will enhance their learning and be useful throughout their lives, and
- celebrating with them their learning successes and encouraging them to continue to build on what they have learned.

To find out how, read on.

ONE

Plasticity and Potential

Connecting Research on the Developing Mind and Brain to Early Learning

An infant claps in delight in a game of pat-a-cake with her caregiver. Two toddlers build block castles side by side, knock them down with hoots of laughter, and immediately start to build again. A group of 3-year-olds, after hearing a story about busy bees, buzz-buzz-buzz near the flower beds at playtime. A preschooler tucks a teddy bear into a play cradle and shares a favorite book, "reading" with a cadence and inflection that suggest a beloved bedtime ritual.

These commonplace experiences in the everyday lives of young children are the signs of developing minds—the outward evidence of the amazing changes taking place inside their brains in response to input from their environments and their own actions, thoughts, and feelings. Educational neuroscience is a relatively recent focus of scientific inquiry that has developed to investigate, among other phenomena, how the brain changes as a result of learning and what these findings might mean for more effective teaching. Brain-imaging techniques and psychological, social, cognitive, and education studies contribute evidence that educational neuroscientists can use to deepen understanding about how human beings learn and develop. In this chapter, we explore findings from this emerging field that are especially relevant for early childhood educators, parents, and caregivers.

1

OUR "PLASTIC" BRAINS

In the late 19th century in his *Principles of Psychology* (1890), William James underscored the importance of the "plasticity" of the nervous system (at least for the young). He positioned education as a significant aspect of society, a place for habits to be learned through a well-organized scheme. This idea about the ability of the nervous system to change in response to learning was largely ignored for decades, as the majority of scientists agreed that the brain changed a great deal in infancy and early childhood as part of normal human development, but those changes slowed down in adolescence and were complete by adulthood.

It is true that "during the first year of life, the brain of an infant is teeming with structural activity as neurons grow in size and complexity and trillions of new connections are formed between them" (Meltzoff, Kuhl, Movellan, & Sejnowski, 2009, p. 284). In recent decades, the development of neuroimaging technologies has enabled scientists to better understand that the structure and function of the brain changes throughout life. As a result, we now know that the brain continues to develop beyond infancy and even adolescence. The term **brain plasticity** is used to describe the changeability of neurons and the structures (**synapses**) that connect these brain cells.

Two Types of Synaptogenesis

Our brains create new synapses through a process called **synaptogenesis**. Scientists have identified two types of synaptic development, referred to as experience *expectant* and experience *dependent*. **Experience-expectant plasticity** refers to experiences that are common to all humans and are important for typical development, such as learning to walk and talk. These types of experiences typically happen early in life and are apt to take place during "**sensitive periods**" of brain and body development. For example, even before they begin speaking, infants' brains are amassing the nuances of how words are pronounced. Exposure to speech in the first 10 months of life is a sensitive period of language development during which infants "acquire the sound prototypes of languages" (Centre for Educational Research and Innovation [CERI], 2007, p. 85) that will determine the accent they adopt when they begin speaking and that will likely persist throughout their lives. Brain research suggests that these sensitive periods coincide with peak periods of synaptic development

(Lightfoot, Cole, & Cole, 2008). The first few years of a child's life are one such period of rapid synaptic growth.

The other type of synaptic development, called **experience-dependent synaptogenesis**, happens throughout life in response to our experiences with people, places, and things around us. These experiences and the synapses that form as a result of these experiences are what make each brain as unique as a fingerprint. Shonkoff and Phillips explain that "experience-dependent brain development is a source of enduring plasticity and of adaptability to the demands of everyday life" (2000, p. 190).

One example of experience-dependent synaptogenesis is vocabulary development, which corresponds to individuals' exposure to language throughout their lives. As we will see in Chapter 5, young children's early exposure to language experiences is a key factor in determining their reading readiness. And throughout their lives, people who read regularly for pleasure or as a work requirement develop an ever-expanding vocabulary. Skills that are developed through practice, like playing a musical instrument or a sport, provide other common examples of experience-dependent plasticity.

Eliot (1999) describes plasticity as the brain "literally being molded by experience," explaining that "every sight, sound, and thought leaves an imprint on specific neural circuits, modifying the way future sights, sounds, and thoughts will be registered" (p. 4). In short, repeated exposure to experiences, such as hearing people talk and learning to wield objects such as blocks and crayons, makes brain connections stronger. The brain also eliminates synapses through a process called **pruning**, through which neural connections created as a result of experiences that are not repeated are eliminated. Pruning does not detract from brain development; it is just part of the developmental process that allows frequently used information to be stored in long-term **memory** more efficiently.

Infancy as an Era of "Exuberant Synaptogenesis"

Babies develop new synapses rapidly during infancy. In fact, their synaptic density greatly exceeds that of adults, peaking around 10 months of age. That is why this is one period of brain development said to characterize **"exuberant synaptogenesis"** (Lightfoot et al., 2008). Subsequently, the number of synapses declines through pruning until the age of 10, when the brain reaches the adult level of synapses (CERI, 2007).

Rushton, Juola-Rushton, and Larkin (2010) put these findings about synaptogenesis in an educational context: "Each day our children leave our classrooms with new synaptic connections and a changed **cerebral cortex**" (p. 352). The brain continues to produce and eliminate synapses throughout life, but the majority of its development occurs during the first 20 years. In the first half of this development process, we learn "how to be *a human being*—learning to move, to communicate, and to master basic social skills" (Sylwester, 2010, p. 60).

In particular, children's brains develop in response to sensory input so that they can comprehend and react to their environment. The senses can be viewed as "the gateway to learning," because sight, hearing, taste, smell, and touch provide input to the brain that permits infants and young children to experience the world around them and learn from it. Early childhood is unparalleled in the breadth of learning that takes place: Reacting and responding to the world around them, infants learn how to communicate, how to grasp and manipulate objects, how to crawl and then walk. This breathtaking pace of mastering new skills continues in early childhood. However, the notion that everything important in brain development occurs in the early years of life is not true. There is no compelling evidence that synaptic development in infancy dictates learning ability later in life (Bruer, 1999).

In fact, experience-dependent brain development occurs throughout life. Neuroscientists have conducted a variety of studies in recent decades demonstrating how various types of learning affect brain development in different ways. For example, brain scans of violinists showed changes in the organization of the cortex, a brain area connected to many types of learning, as a result of their intensive music practice (Hinton, Fischer, & Glennon, 2012). Research involving London cabdrivers showed that the hippocampal areas of their brains, associated with spatial reasoning, were larger than those of other adults. And the longer a cabdriver had been navigating the streets of London, the larger his or her hippocampus was likely to be. German scientists conducted scans of the brains of medical students before they began studying for their professional exams and again when they took those tests; their gray matter volume—the number of neurons and synaptic connections—increased measurably over those three months of study (Draganski et al., 2006). The subjects of these studies developed remarkable gains in musical ability, navigation skills, and medical knowledge through a great deal of study and practice—and their hard work and learning actually changed their brains and made them smarter.

Settling the Nature vs. Nurture Debate?

Plasticity research has shed new light on the long-running debate about whether human capabilities are primarily the product of our genetic endowment (nature) or the environment and opportunities to which we are exposed (nurture). Researchers now agree that we develop based on a complex interaction between our genes and the environment. "The genes that a baby inherits from her parents do not determine exactly what kind of person she will become, but they do define the range of possible developmental outcomes that are open to her" (Aamodt & Wang, 2011, p. 35). At the same time, our environment helps to determine the extent to which we achieve our potential.

Sylwester (2010) concludes that "parents and educators can't change the genetic history of a child, but they can do the kind of nurturing that will provide the child with the best possible adaptations of whatever nature provided" (p. 18). Furthermore, parents and teachers should bear in mind that each child's brain, because it develops through this complex interaction, is unique (Hinton et al., 2012)—and so should be the educational opportunities presented to help each child learn and thrive. A budding violinist doesn't become a great musician because she was born with a big cortex; that area of her brain develops as a result of music lessons, guidance from effective teachers, and her own dedication to practice, practice, and more practice.

This blend of genetic and environmental influences also determines what neuroscience researcher Richard Davidson calls our Emotional Style—our resilience when confronted with setbacks, our capacity to sustain positive emotion over time, our abilities to interpret our own feelings and those of others, our sensitivity to context, and our ability to focus our attention. "Genetic propensities can aim a child down a path that leads to a particular Emotional Style, but certain experiences and environments can move the child off that path and onto another" (Davidson, 2012, p. 93). He explains that some experiences that shape our brains are generated externally, but because we control our thoughts and intentions, "by mental activity alone, we can intentionally change our own brain" (p. 162). These exciting findings from neuroscience support, for example, the premise of Chapter 4, that parents and early childhood educators can guide young children to develop an optimistic outlook about their ability to learn, to grow their knowledge and skills, and to achieve the goals they set for themselves.

CONNECTING PLASTICITY TO CHILDREN'S POTENTIAL TO LEARN AND GROW

What the research about brain plasticity tells us is that the environment—in the form of opportunities and support for learning—has a significant impact on how children develop. Rather than thinking about children's potential to learn as being dictated by their genetic makeup, we can see that every child should be able to learn if given access to appropriate learning experiences. Educational philosopher Israel Scheffler (2010) identifies a pervasive idea in American society that academic ability is a stable, fixed trait, that some children are naturally gifted with the ability to learn while others are not, and that the best efforts of teachers and students cannot influence innate intellect. Scheffler makes the case for redefining potential as the capacity to acquire new skills and knowledge—and we know from recent advances in neuroscience that brain plasticity gives all of us the capacity to learn.

By building on this definition, we can understand learning potential as the capacity for acquiring the knowledge and skills to achieve to a higher level of performance in any area. Potential is not represented by a child's inherent skill in some domain, nor is there any guarantee that a child will achieve his or her potential. In order to do so, the proper conditions for success must be present: a safe and encouraging environment that provides ample opportunities for a child to learn new information and practice new skills. As Hinton and colleagues (2012) put it:

> The educational environment plays a crucial role in shaping the brain's abilities and determining students' academic achievement. Education should therefore strive to provide learning experiences that enable students at all levels to build toward mastery of a common set of skills. (p. 5)

Rethinking potential and recognizing that most all children have the capacity to learn can have a profound effect on the expectations educators set for the children in their charge—and on children's own beliefs in their abilities. Higher expectations and more positive beliefs, in turn, affect educational outcomes. In inspirational movies, when young people are told they don't have what it takes to succeed, they rise up and prove their detractors wrong. In real life, unfortunately, children too often conform to low expectations that parents and teachers have about their learning ability (Hattie, 2009).

The good news is that when caring adults have high expectations for children and model optimism about their ability to accomplish learning tasks, achievement may increase. In addition, classroom studies (Dweck, 2006) show that when students are taught that intelligence is not fixed—that they can make themselves smarter and change their brains—they are more likely to persist in learning tasks until they succeed, and this success fuels continued progress. Optimism about one's ability to succeed is as crucial for young children as it is for school-age youth. This power of positivity is so important that we devote an entire chapter to teaching and modeling an optimistic outlook.

STAGES OF DEVELOPMENT

Although infant and early child development proceeds differently for each child, it may be useful here to summarize the parts of the brain and types of **cognitive development** that are most active in early childhood. Hannaford (2005) formulated this outline as one model of developmental stages:

Conception to 15 months: Brainstem

- Basic survival needs: food, shelter, security, and safety
- Sensory development: vestibular, hearing, tactile, smell, taste, and vision
- Motor: basic reflexes to motor exploration

15 months to 4½ years: Limbic system (developing awareness of relationships and social abilities)

- Understanding of self/others, self/emotions, and self/language
- Exploration: emotional, language, imagination, gross motor, memory, and social

4½ to 7 years: Gestalt elaboration

- Whole picture processing/cognition
- Image, movement, rhythm, emotion, intuition

7 to 9 years: Analytic and frontal lobe elaboration

- Detail and linear processing, cognition, control of social behavior
- Refinement of elements of language, inner speech
- Technique development: music, art, sports, dance, manual training
- Fine motor and eye teaming for tracking and two-dimensional focus
- Reading and writing skills development, and linear math processing

LEARNING THROUGH IMITATION
AND THE ROLE OF MIRROR NEURONS

At each of these developmental stages, infants and young children are learning from the world around them. They learn a great deal by imitating the actions and, later, the speech of others. From the work of well-known theorist and social psychologist Albert Bandura (1977), we know that opportunities for observation and imitation increase the probability that children will learn new behaviors. For decades, psychologist Andrew Meltzoff has been studying the phenomenon of infants and young children learning through imitation. In a 1997 study, Meltzoff and fellow researcher M. Keith Moore reported that newborns just hours and days old (the earliest experiment was 42 minutes after birth) mimicked adults sticking out their tongues. Learning through imitation extends to much more than simple actions. Based on these and other studies, Meltzoff developed the "Like Me" hypothesis, which holds that by imitating the actions of others, infants and young children come to relate those actions to their own mental states and then to the internal states of others. Meltzoff writes:

> Human adults and children effortlessly learn new behaviors from watching others. Parents provide their young with an apprenticeship in how to act as a member of their particular culture long before verbal instruction is possible. A wide range of behaviors—from tool use to social customs—are passed from one generation to another through imitative learning. (2005, p. 55)

What Meltzoff and his colleagues have observed in studies with children, neuroscientists have seen at work in the brains of animal subjects. **Mirror neurons** are special cells in the brain that are activated when we see someone doing something. In effect, our brain responds as if our body were doing the same action. This virtual mimicry may have crucial implications for teaching young children through demonstration.

Iacoboni (2009) has identified a network of human brain regions with cells that have mirror neuron properties. He states that "solid empirical evidence suggests that our brains are capable of mirroring the deepest aspects of the minds of others . . . at the fine grained level of a single brain cell" (p. 7). Mirror neurons are most active when we see someone performing an action right in front of us. Thus, it follows that these cells are working full-time in the brains of infants as they spend most of their time observing—and learning from—the actions of adults and other children around them.

Mirror neurons were first identified by a team of researchers led by Giacomo Rizzolatti at University of Parma, Italy, in the 1990s. The researchers were studying monkeys that had wires implanted into their brains to record which parts of the brain carried out planning and movement. A team member noticed that when he ate a peanut in front of a monkey, the same neurons in the monkey's brain were activated as if it were bringing a peanut to its mouth (Blakeslee, 2006).

Meltzoff and Moore suggest that learning through imitation ultimately plays a key role in the development of social cognition, which refers to how we process, store, and use information about other people, how we come to understand them. What children learn through imitation includes "taking the perspective of others, role-taking and, eventually, the uniquely human capacity to form moral judgements based on the fundamental equality of persons" (1997, p. 190).

Research into the implications of mirror neurons for education continues. For example, scientists are studying whether these neurons are present at birth or whether they develop in response to observation, imitation, and learning. As this research continues, we can build on the capabilities of infants and young children to learn through imitation. By observing parents, caregivers, teachers, older siblings, and others, young children follow their actions and, ultimately, may learn to read the intentions of others.

Eventually, learning expands to take in several steps of an action and translates into anticipating what will happen next. For example, as adults, if someone reaches for toys to put into a bucket, we will look at the bucket before the hand reaches the bucket with the toys. We can predict what is going to happen: If we were doing the action ourselves, our eyes would look at the bucket before our hand places the toys inside it. Infants who are 6 months old do not anticipate with their eyes where somebody's hand will place the toys, but by 1 year of age, babies *can* do this, just as adults can (Iacoboni, 2009). This progression indicates that the brain is learning to predict the actions and intent of other people.

Sylwester (2010) suggests that mirror neurons may be at work as infants babble in response to their parents speaking **motherese**, the exaggerated and repetitive speech patterns that many adults naturally adopt in talking with babies: "Over time, in a verbal environment, the child begins to correctly utter simple phonemic combinations . . . and eventually, smooth articulate speech emerges" (p. 25). Imagine the applications of learning through imitation at work when caregivers and parents read regularly to their children and when children see adults and older children reading for pleasure.

In conjunction with our earlier discussion about positive expectations, it is crucial to emphasize that research to date has found that mirror neurons activate in response to both physical actions and emotional stimuli. Young children are sensitive to the moods and emotions of their parents, caregivers, and teachers. If you stick your tongue out at an infant in play, he will respond in kind. If you smile, he smiles back. As Rushton and colleagues (2010) explain:

> At a subliminal level, children observe the teacher's expression and dispositions and internalize how the teacher is feeling. Neuroscientists believe that our ability to empathize with another human being is due, in part, to the activation of the mirror neuron networks being activated by what we observe. (p. 355)

These findings reinforce the importance of establishing and maintaining a positive, caring environment in which children feel safe, secure, valued, and encouraged to enjoy learning.

LEARNING IN THE EARLY YEARS:
BECOMING "THE BOSS OF YOUR BRAIN"

The brains of infants and young children are always "on," taking in and processing stimuli from the people in their lives and surrounding environment. As Hawley (2000) notes, the brain is "the most immature of all organs at birth" (p. 2); it grows and develops based on an infant's interactions with people and objects around him or her. The value of this immaturity is that it allows "initial learning to influence the developing neural architecture in ways that support later, more complex learning" (Meltzoff et al., 2009, p. 284); this explosion of neural activity is known as "exuberant learning." In other words, the early experiences of infants and toddlers form the neural connections that facilitate the development of language, problem-solving, social, and motor skills.

For the young child, learning and play are the same thing. Learning is a joyful experience that immerses the child in a challenging learning process involving intellect, creativity, emotions, and physiology. Education occurs in a variety of settings, not just in a formal classroom environment. Time spent at home in informal learning, on the playground, and in other nontraditional learning experiences offers many opportunities for children to develop new knowledge and skills.

While each child's brain is unique, the vast majority of children are equipped with exceptional features that allow them to explore the world around them and learn from it (Caine, Caine, Klimek, & McClintic, 2008):

- the ability to detect patterns and to make approximations,
- an extensive capacity for various types of memory,
- the ability to self-correct and learn from experience by the way of analysis of external data and self-reflection, and
- an inexhaustible capacity to create.

The human brain collects information about the world and organizes it to form a representation about the world. This representation, or mental model, describes thinking, a process people use to function in the world. Humans are born with brains that have all the sensory components and neural organization necessary to survive successfully in their environments. A crucial question for parents and early childhood educators is this: Can we teach young children to think more productively?

In the same way that children can be guided to develop their large and small motor skills, they can be taught to build their "mental muscles" by learning to use **critical thinking** and problem-solving strategies. For example, young children can be taught how to organize content—by comparing and grouping like objects and using mnemonics, for example—to promote more efficient thinking (Gazzaniga, 1989). On a larger scale, parents and educators can guide and encourage children to develop **self-control**, which Aamodt and Wang (2011) call "the best gift you can give," noting that "preschool children's ability to resist temptation is a much better predictor of eventual academic success than their IQ scores" (p. 112). A study of eighth-grade students showed the continuing importance of self-discipline during school years, with the results revealing that the more self-disciplined students outperformed their less-disciplined peers on a variety of academic criteria such as better grades on report cards, higher standardized achievement test scores, and better school attendance (Duckworth & Seligman, 2005).

Self-control is one aspect of a range of higher-order thinking skills under the umbrella of **executive function**, the set of cognitive processes we use to organize our thoughts and activities, set priorities, and manage time to accomplish the goals we set for ourselves. Executive function emanates from the prefrontal region of the brain's frontal lobe, which has been associated with organizational abilities, verbal fluency, working memory, control of emotions, and social skills (Goldberg, 2009).

It is possible to guide children to harness the power of their executive function, to begin to become "the boss of their brains" (Wilson & Conyers, 2011b). The term **metacognition** refers to thinking about one's thinking with the aim of identifying strategies useful for solving the problem at hand and of improving one's use of those strategies. This way of thinking about thinking may be beyond the reach of young children, but we can see early stages of metacognition at work when 4- and 5-year-olds define goals ("Let's build a tower just like that one!") and monitor their progress toward achievement ("We should start over and build it bigger at the bottom").

Children can learn thinking skills—we call them "cognitive assets"—to support their creative and problem-solving endeavors. Over the long term, research shows that explicit instruction on cognitive and metacognitive strategies enhances student achievement (Bransford, Brown, & Cocking, 2000; Hattie, 2009). Thus, modeling and guiding young children in the use of these strategies sends an early message that they are in charge of their learning and supports the notion that they can get smarter.

We discuss the role of **self-regulation** in early childhood development and present several examples of useful cognitive assets throughout this text in sections titled "Learning How to Learn." These sections are accompanied by stories featuring engaging animal characters demonstrating cognitive skills in action. You can share these stories with young children and introduce related activities to guide them to begin using these thinking and problem-solving skills.

AEIOU: THE LEARNING CYCLE

These early years are the beginning of a life of learning, an endeavor that certainly starts with a bang! As we have seen in this chapter, neuroscientists and psychologists describe both the synaptic development that takes place early in life and the learning intertwined with it as "exuberant." We can synthesize what is known about how the brain learns into the **AEIOU learning cycle,** with five stages represented by the vowels *a, e, i, o,* and *u* (Wilson, Heverly, & Conyers, 2011) for awareness, exploration, inquiry, order, and understanding or use. Developing your understanding of this learning cycle may deepen your appreciation for the learning that may take place in even the most mundane and frivolous of activities: making a game out of picking up toys in the play area, dressing up for pretend play, or making up a story about where the butterfly goes after it flies over the fence. Consider the example in Table 1.1.

This cycle of learning occurs daily throughout our lives as the human brain becomes aware of new knowledge, concepts, information, and skills. As parents and educators, we can encourage young children to embrace these learning opportunities by providing safe, positive, and enriching environments with appropriate levels of challenge that promote progressively more complex learning, application, and use of knowledge. We also advocate calling attention to learning, explicitly modeling and guiding children to develop cognitive abilities that will aid in learning, and celebrating learning gains. As supported by the stages of development presented earlier in this chapter, children learn from whole to parts, from concrete to abstract, and from simple to complex.

Table 1.1.   AEIOU in Action: Problem Solving

A	Awareness	*A young child notices something new.* Eager to go outside, he grabs his shoes and puts them on. Voila! He can dress himself. His caregiver notices and gives him a big smile: "Look at you! Putting on your own shoes!"
E	Exploration	*The child explores the concept.* As he runs outside, he realizes that something feels odd about his left shoe. His toes feel like there's not enough room for them.
I	Inquiry	*The child develops an inquiry.* The child runs to his caregiver and says, "My shoe feels funny." Together, they look at his feet. The caregiver asks, "What's different?" The child notices he can see his sock under the Velcro strap of his left shoe, but not his right. The caregiver says, "Your tongue is missing," which makes him laugh. She explains that shoes have tongues, too.
O	Order	*The child puts the concept into some order.* The child takes off both shoes and sees that the tongue of his left shoe is pushed up into the toe. He pulls it out so that it looks like his right shoe. Then he puts them both on more carefully. Now both shoes feel good, and he runs off to play.
U	Understanding/ Use	*The child puts his new understanding to use.* The child puts his own shoes on every day now. One day a friend puts her own shoes on, too, following his example. But she says they feel funny. He looks down and exclaims, "Your tongues are missing!" They both laugh. Then he shows his friend how to keep her tongues straight.

Supporting AEIOU in Action

This cycle of learning itself is not intended as a subject for explicit instruction to young children. However, it may be helpful to guide children through these steps and take advantage when opportunities present themselves to point out the usefulness of

- focusing awareness on and exploring new things and ideas,
- pursuing inquiries, and
- bringing order to and continuing to enhance understanding of what they have learned by applying it in new situations.

In the scenario in Table 1.1, for example, the caregiver guides a child to develop an inquiry about the proper way to put on his shoes, and he later mirrors this guidance in sharing his knowledge with a friend. Throughout this text, we will share other examples of how you can guide children to apply one or more of the AEIOU components to learning opportunities that arise naturally as they play and explore the world around them.

Cultivating Potential

These aspects of how the minds and brains of young children develop can help to inform your efforts to create and maintain a positive learning environment for young children:

Playtime is learning time. Hinton and colleagues (2012) emphasize that "active engagement is a prerequisite for the changes in brain circuitry that are thought to underlie learning. In educational terms, this suggests that passively sitting in a classroom hearing a teacher lecture will not necessarily lead to learning" (p. 5). Active learning is even more crucial for young children. Toward that end, you may choose to do the following:

- Rotate boxes of toys, building sets, and manipulatives in the play area that coincide with books you read during story time. For example, a box of plastic bugs and farm animals will likely be popular if you are reading *Charlotte's Web*.
- Emphasize the hands-on aspects of learning. If you are reading books about outer space, for example, it may be more engaging to keep the inflatable planets, stars, moons, and sun in a bin in the play area rather than hanging them from the ceiling out of children's reach.
- Offer variety. Some children enjoy learning by building with blocks or creating with clay, while others prefer pretend play with dress-up and props.

Learning is incremental. Brain plasticity research suggests that learning is an ongoing process, as the learning cycle is repeated with increasingly sophisticated outcomes. A child learns to put on his own shoes and then helps a friend do the same. Those abilities produce confidence and the motor skills to take on progressively tougher tasks, like buttoning a sweater, zipping a coat, and tying new shoes. To support incremental learning, you may do the following:

- Give children plenty of practice with basic skills so they can experience success and master the abilities they will need to take on harder tasks.
- Emphasize learning as a step-by-step process so that children come to understand that they can achieve a big goal by accomplishing smaller tasks along the way.
- Once children have mastered basic skills, challenge them to take the next step.

You are the lead learner. Children love to follow the leader, and when it comes to learning, that leader is you! You can embrace your role as a model learner by doing the following:

- Think out loud. For example, build a rickety tower and then talk through the ways you might make it better: "Maybe if I make the base bigger, I can make a higher tower."
- Emphasize that you learn new things, too. "So a spider isn't a bug? I didn't know that!"
- Ask questions, encourage children to suggest solutions, and follow their lead. "When we turn over the bucket, the sand just flows out. I wonder how we could make it hold its shape?"
- Set realistic, high expectations for your children and yourself, and celebrate successes along the way.

TWO

Ten Facts About the Amazing Human Brain

1 Infant Brain = 100 Billion to 200 Billion Neurons

2 Brain Hemispheres Work Together to Support Thinking

3 Brain Systems Process Specialized Functions

4 Lobes Facilitate Input and Output

5 Senses Connect the Brain to the Environment

6 Dimensions of Emotional Style Serve as Building Blocks

7 States of Consciousness Form an Infant's Daily Cycle

8 Forms of Intelligence Develop as Young Children Explore the World

9 Elements Help Define an Infant's Temperament

10 Million Books = Brain Capacity

The brain is the body's control center—in charge of all aspects of operating a living creature, from controlling basic functions such as heart rate and breathing to accepting and interpreting input from the senses to facilitating thought and the experience of emotions. The human brain is a marvel in its ability to take in and process new information. This neuroplasticity—the brain's capability to adapt to changes and new information by forming new neural connections throughout life—powers infants' and young children's growing comprehension of the world around them. Let's explore 10 key facts about the brain to establish a foundation for the amazing learning potential of young children.

17

1 INFANT BRAIN = 100 BILLION TO 200 BILLION NEURONS

At birth, the human brain has billions of brain cells, called **neurons**—various estimates put this number at 100 billion to 200 billion—and 1 *trillion* **glial cells**, which provide support and nutrition to neurons. These neurons form more than 50 trillion connections, which are called **synapses**, with other neurons. As Woolfolk (2010) puts it, infants and toddlers "are *oversupplied* with the neurons and synapses that they will need to adapt to their environments" (p. 29, emphasis in original text). All this activity indicates a brain already hard at work learning from the surrounding world. As Aamodt and Wang note, "Your baby is smarter than he or she lets on. For generations, the slow development of motor systems led psychologists to believe that babies had very simple mental lives" (2011, p. 2). We are learning from educational neuroscience that, soon after birth, the infant brain is so busy learning that it consumes 60% of the baby's energy intake (Meltzoff et al., 2009, p. 284).

By age 3, a child has twice as many connections between neurons as his or her parents (Johnson, 2009). These will be pruned down, and the most-used synaptic connections will remain as the child ages through adulthood. Neurons send out branches to connect with many other neurons, and these branches are either **axons** (which send information out) or **dendrites** (which take information in). Stamm (2007) offers this analogy:

> The newborn brain is like a communication network in a city where the main lines in each neighborhood exist, but time and experiences are required to create specific connections from house to house. Each brain begins to make its own unique associations with wires that literally grow themselves as needed. (p. 16)

Research has established that experiences after birth, rather than a genetic blueprint, determine the actual "wiring" of the human brain. In effect, cells that fire together wire together and form permanent connections (Hebb, 1949). Research by Peter Huttenlocher, a neurobiologist formerly with the University of Chicago, showed that a tissue sample from a 28-week-old fetal brain had 124 million connections, a newborn sample had 253 million connections, and an 8-month-old infant had 572 million connections. This growth slows down by the end of the first year and stabilizes at about 354 million connections. Huttenlocher's studies (2002) indicate that the fetal brain overproduces cells, but unless they find a connection or a "job" to perform, these cells die.

The brains of infants and toddlers are highly adaptable, as many of the specific brain regions have not yet decided on specific functions they will take on. As Eliot (1999) explains, the initial wiring of a particular brain region during the period of synaptic overproduction marks the onset of a particular ability, such as vision in an infant's first few months and language in the second year. However, the prolonged "pruning" period that follows fixes the overall quality of each ability, because this is when neural activity preserves the most-used connections, thus wiring the brain for certain ways of thinking, perceiving, and acting.

2 BRAIN HEMISPHERES WORK TOGETHER TO SUPPORT THINKING

The human body is fairly balanced in its construction, with an eye, an ear, an arm, and a leg for the most part evenly spaced on each side of the body from a line of symmetry that runs from the top of the head to the feet. This symmetry is reflected in the structure of the brain as well, which is divided into a right hemisphere and a left hemisphere. The two **brain hemispheres** are connected by a band of nerve fibers called the **corpus callosum**.

Though they are near mirror structures, the two hemispheres have some specialized functions. Portions of the left hemisphere are heavily involved in language, math, and logic processing, while the right hemisphere supports spatial abilities and facial recognition. But even though some thinking abilities seem to be dominant in one hemisphere or the other, both sides contribute to overall brain activity. As Zimmer (2011) notes, "the left hemisphere specializes in picking out the sounds that form words and working out the syntax of the words, for example, but it does not have a monopoly on language processing" (p. 70). The left and right hemispheres function in tandem to accomplish most daily tasks (Torrance & Olson, 2009). Within the context of child development and the brain, the left and right hemispheres work together to support the development of language and problem-solving abilities.

In several much-studied cases, neurologists disconnected the brain hemispheres to eliminate debilitating seizures in patients with severe epilepsy (Immordino-Yang & Fischer, 2007). With extensive support and therapy, these patients have, to varying degrees, been able to "retrain" their brains to take over some of the functions previously handled by one or the other hemisphere. The fact that the brain can so extensively rewire is a dramatic example of neuroplasticity at work. It also refutes the notion that some people are "left-brain" thinkers (and thus more rational) while others are "right-brain" thinkers (reacting primarily with their emotions). In fact, many neurons have their cell nucleus in one hemisphere while their extensions are in the other; this and other evidence suggests that most cognitive tasks require that the two hemispheres work together (CERI, 2007).

3 BRAIN SYSTEMS PROCESS SPECIALIZED FUNCTIONS

The brain can be described as a "triune" of three systems (MacLean, 1990; Newman & Harris, 2009):

- the **neocortex**, which deals with higher-order information processing;
- the **limbic system**, which deals with emotions; and
- the **brainstem**, sometimes referred to as the "reptilian" part of the brain, which deals with the basic instincts of survival (e.g., finding nourishment) and defense ("fight, flight, or freeze").

The limbic system encompasses the neural network for behaviors of attachment between parents and infants, including nursing, vocalizations to maintain contact, and play. The limbic system may also play a role in maintaining the sense of personal being and the conviction that we attach to our beliefs, and it may be activated in evaluating the significance of incoming information.

The brain operates differently when any type of threat is perceived by relying more on the use of faster, survival-oriented responses of the brainstem and less on the higher-order thinking skills of the neocortex (Neve, Hart, & Thomas, 1986). Threats may take the form of physical harm or emotional upset. Threats cause the brain to feel fear, mistrust, anxiety, or general helplessness. We feel stressed when we feel helpless because we do not see a solution to a problem, lack the resources to solve a problem, or have little or no control over a problem.

Helpless babies need food, warmth, and comfort, so they learn to signal their parents to provide for those needs. Parents and caregivers need to create an environment for infants that is safe, nurturing, and relaxed. Fostering a positive outlook is also crucial as infants grow into toddlers. When caring adults model positive emotions, young children mirror that outlook and are more likely to develop an optimistic outlook about life and learning (Wilson & Conyers, 2011a).

4 LOBES FACILITATE INPUT AND OUTPUT

Each of the brain's two hemispheres has four divisions, or "lobes." From front to back, those lobes are

- the **frontal lobe**, the largest section, which encompasses the **pre-frontal cortex** (involved in formulating plans and strategies for behavior, making complex judgments, directing and sustaining attention, and inhibiting impulses) and the **motor cortex** (which receives information from other parts of the brain and uses this information to carry out body movements);
- the **temporal lobe**, involved in hearing, memory, and understanding language, time, and spatial relationships (because of its connection to the limbic system, the temporal lobe also plays a critical role in emotions);
- the **parietal lobe**, which receives input from sensory receptors to provide information about touch, pain, pressure, and temperature; and
- the **occipital lobe**, which is involved primarily in the ability to see and perceive visual information.

5 SENSES CONNECT THE BRAIN TO THE ENVIRONMENT

The brain uses all five senses to learn: seeing, hearing, touching, tasting, and smelling.

Seeing

- Babies appear to come with "preloaded software devoted to visual processing" and "display a preference for patterns with high contrast" (Medina, 2008, p. 235).
- A 6- to 8-month-old infant has a visual system very much like that of an adult (Stamm, 2007).

- The retina is covered with 120 million to 125 million rod cells and between 6 million and 7 million cone cells for seeing in dim and bright light, respectively (Gibb, 2007).
- The sense of sight plays a crucial role in learning: 72 hours after exposure to information presented verbally, people remember about 10%; if a picture is added to the verbal information, retention increases to 65% (Medina, 2008).

Hearing

- "Our ears provide a complete 360 degree sensory field from which the brain can tell not just the volume and pitch of a sound but the direction and distance of the source" (Gibb, 2007, p. 51).
- Auditory information travels from the nerves in the ears to the brainstem and temporal lobes; the temporal lobes house brain structures that play crucial roles in processing language to extract meaning.

Touch

- The average adult's skin weighs between 6 and 8 pounds and covers about 20 square feet (Idaho Public Television, 2003).
- A section of skin the size of a quarter contains more than 3 million cells, 100–340 sweat glands, 50 nerve endings, and 3 feet of blood vessels (Montagu, 1986).

Taste

- Sensory cells on the tongue discriminate among salty, sweet, bitter, sour, and savory flavors.
- Whereas scientists once believed specific taste buds were localized to specific places on the tongue, we now know that these sensory cells are located all over the tongue (Gibb, 2007).

Smell

- The "olfactory region" is a collection of neurons about the size of a postage stamp that lies between the eyes (Medina, 2008).
- Human beings may have up to 1,000 separate olfactory neurons, each attuned to a highly specific odor (Gibb, 2007).
- Familiar smells can evoke powerful memories and emotions (Rodriguez-Gil, 2004).

The first sensory system to fully develop—at about 5 months—is the **vestibular system**, which controls the sense of movement and balance (Hannaford, 2005). Synapses begin to form in the motor cortex at about 2 months, in the visual cortex at 3 months, and in the **hippocampus** (which controls memory functions) at 8 months (Chugani & Phelps, 1991). By 12 months, a baby's auditory map is formed, with clusters of neurons corresponding to **phonemes** (the smallest unit of language) the infant has heard over and over again from parents, grandparents, siblings, and others (Begley, 1997). Thus, visual, auditory, and tactile stimuli help the infant's brain develop.

6 DIMENSIONS OF EMOTIONAL STYLE SERVE AS BUILDING BLOCKS

Davidson (2012) identifies six aspects of our Emotional Style, the "fundamental building blocks" of our moods and responses to people and experiences. One's Emotional Style "is governed by specific, identifiable brain circuits and can be measured using objective laboratory methods" (p. xi). These dimensions are

- resilience, or how slowly or quickly people recover from an adverse experience;
- outlook, which refers to how long people are able to sustain positive emotions;
- social intuition, the ability to pick up social signals when interacting with or observing others;
- self-awareness about one's feelings that reflect emotions;
- sensitivity to context, or the ability to regulate emotional responses in keeping with experiences and environmental conditions; and
- attention, or people's ability to focus on a chosen task or subject.

In combination, these dimensions may describe various traits. For example, Davidson notes, a person who is impulsive typically exhibits the combination of unfocused attention and low self-awareness; someone who is anxious has an Emotional Style characterized by being slow to recover and having a negative outlook, high level of self-awareness, and low attention; and an optimist is both resilient and has a positive outlook. "Who you are emotionally is the product of different amounts of each of these six components. Because there are so many ways to combine the six dimensions, there are countless Emotional Styles; everyone's is unique" (p. 6). A key point about Emotional Style is that it is not fixed, but can change in response to one's experiences, environmental conditions, and conscious thoughts and intentions, a subject we will explore in more detail in Chapter 4.

7 STATES OF CONSCIOUSNESS FORM AN INFANT'S DAILY CYCLE

British pediatrician Peter Wolff (1987) pinpointed seven states of consciousness that an infant goes through each day. The way a baby moves in and out of these states of consciousness becomes predictable to parents and caregivers. These seven states are

- *State 1* **Regular or deep sleep:** the baby is still, pale, and breathing evenly; in this protected state, the infant is usually curled up and closing out the world.
- *State 2* **Irregular sleep:** the baby moves, jerks, startles, and breathes irregularly; in this state, the baby may awaken sleepily and fussily or struggle to sink into deep sleep.
- *State 3* **Periodic sleep:** alternating bursts of states 1 and 2, which occur when an infant rouses or returns to sleep and is trying to get comfortable.
- *State 4* **Drowsiness:** the infant's eyes begin to droop, giving them a glazed look, and breathing begins to slow in preparation for sleep.
- *State 5* **Alert inactivity:** the baby's body is still, but he or she is looking eagerly at the surroundings; breathing is rapid and irregular.
- *State 6* **Waking activity:** there are spurts of physical activity with lots of twisting and stretching, but without much visual focus.
- *State 7* **Crying:** this activity involves lots of movement, flushing of the skin, wailing, and, later in infancy, tears. There are many types of crying, including a piercing, painful sound; a demanding, urgent cry; a bored-hollow cry; and a rhythmic, but not urgent, cry that happens when an infant is tired or overloaded with sensory stimuli.

Each baby develops an individual pattern of these states, and this pattern or cycle tends to remain relatively constant regardless of the noise and activity around a baby. Wolff recommends that parents and caregivers plan activities for infants around these states. For example, state 6 is the best time to let a baby move, squirm, wiggle, and play. The best time to put a baby to bed is at the beginning of stage 4 rather than waiting for state 7. Infants are most ready to learn at state 5, which is thus the best time to read to them because they are most interested in looking and listening.

8 FORMS OF INTELLIGENCE DEVELOP AS YOUNG CHILDREN EXPLORE THE WORLD

Howard Gardner's popular theory proposes that the brain uses multiple intelligences rather than a single, fixed intelligence (2006). He defines intelligence as the human ability to solve problems or to make something that is valued in one or more cultures. As a result, Gardner's question is no longer "How smart am I?" but "How am I smart?" The eight forms of intelligence framed by Gardner are the following:

1. mathematical/logical—the ability to solve problems (excel at math, fix, repair, troubleshoot);
2. verbal/linguistic—ability to use language (reading, writing, speaking, explaining);
3. interpersonal—ability to understand other people (social skills, building relationships);
4. intrapersonal—ability to understand yourself and know who you are (introspection, self-reflection, self-assessment);
5. musical/rhythmic—ability to think in music (clapping, drumming, composing, playing music);
6. spatial—ability to represent the spatial world internally (art and sciences, architecture, navigation);
7. bodily/kinesthetic—ability in excellent body control (dance, athletics, juggling, musical performance); and
8. naturalistic—discrimination among living things and sensitivity to the natural world (botany, environmental sciences)

Gardner's work on multiple intelligences continues to evolve, as the addition of naturalistic intelligence to the original list of seven domains demonstrates.

Of the view of multiple intelligences, Gardner writes:

It is of the utmost importance that we recognize and nurture all of the varied human intelligences and all of the combinations of intelligences.

> We are all so different largely because we have different combinations of intelligences. If we recognize this, I think we will have at least a better chance of dealing appropriately with the many problems that we face in the world. (2006, p. 24)

In his 1995 book, *A Celebration of Neurons*, Robert Sylwester discusses the possibilities of measuring and charting seven of Gardner's forms of intelligence by assessing whether the following groups of intelligences are areas of strength or weakness for each child.

Time/Sequence

- Linguistic
- Musical
- Mathematical/logical

Space/Place

- Spatial
- Bodily/kinesthetic

Personal/Social

- Intrapersonal
- Interpersonal

For optimal learning and an optimistic outlook, it is important to recognize the capabilities and individual differences of each child. By exposing children to each type of ability, we enable them to capitalize on their preferences, capabilities, and talents. Understanding these eight intelligences in a child can help parents and educators determine how best to present learning tasks and information in a way that the child can acquire knowledge and skills rapidly and with ease. This approach helps the child succeed and gives him or her the opportunity to be an active participant in learning activities.

9 ELEMENTS HELP DEFINE AN INFANT'S TEMPERAMENT

In their classic New York longitudinal study that began in the early 1950s, Thomas and Chess (1977) identified nine elements that can be used to describe an infant's temperament.

1. Activity level: Is the infant very active or quiet?
2. Distractibility: How does the infant focus?

3. Persistence: Does the infant continue to try or give up in challenges?

4. Approach–withdrawal: How does the infant handle new and stressful situations?

5. Intensity: How intense are the infant's reactions and responses?

6. Adaptability: How does the infant deal with change and transition?

7. Regularity: How predictable are the infant's patterns, cycles, and habits?

8. Sensory threshold: How does the child react to various sensory stimuli?

9. Mood: Does the infant react with basically positive or negative responses?

An infant's temperament and emotional development are modulated by the brain and his or her perception of individual experiences. The tendencies and signs of temperament—how a child responds to the world around him or her—are observable by 6 weeks of age. By 7 months, a baby's temperament or personality is established enough that parents and other caregivers have a framework to judge his or her reactions as typical and expected. As a result, they can assess that an infant is his or her "usual self."

The differences in temperament exhibited by infants and young children are one outward manifestation of their unique brains. But in the same way that intelligence is malleable (see Chapter 1), temperament should not be viewed as a rigidly fixed trait. These characteristics can and will change over years of maturation and development. The same is true for the multiple intelligences identified by Gardner (2006), as outlined in the previous section; children may exhibit an early strength in one area of intelligence, but through guidance, learning, and persistent effort they can develop other intelligences as well.

10 MILLION BOOKS = BRAIN CAPACITY

In his book *The Owner's Manual for the Brain* (1999), Howard estimates that the human brain has the capacity to store the equivalent of 10 million books. The brain learns and processes all this data through stimulation, experience, and behavior. In effect, new information stimulates the brain to form new neural connections that tuck what is learned away for future reference. Brain research using a PET scan indicates that many areas of the brain "light up" when presented with a new task; once that task is learned and repeated, less of the brain is activated (Van Mier, Tempel, Perlmutter, Raichle, & Petersen, 1998). This research demonstrates how quickly the brain adapts and rewires itself to learn and store information.

The brain begins customizing itself with learned information from the day a child is born. Early in a child's life, parents and other caregivers need to provide a variety of sensory experiences to stimulate learning and develop the potential of the infant brain. A brain-friendly environment for infants and toddlers continually presents learning challenges, new information, and the opportunity for young children to interact with caring adults and other children as they process new experiences. Frequent exposure to new learning experiences and challenges are critical to brain growth and have a direct impact on the various forms of intelligence.

Of course, we cannot peer directly into the brains of infants and toddlers as they develop, but various types of brain research support the importance of learning throughout life. For example, a group of neuroscientists conducted brain autopsies on graduate students and high school dropouts; they found 40% more neural connections in the brains of graduate students (Gregory & Parry, 2006). This type of research quantifies the physical changes in the brain that correspond to an environment rich in opportunities to learn—and the earlier children are exposed to this environment, the better.

☆PRACTICAL TIPS FOR EARLY CHILDHOOD EDUCATORS☆

Cultivating Your Knowledge About the Brain

More has been learned about the brain in the last decade than in the past 200 years (Restak, 2009). These discoveries have given rise to the field of educational neuroscience, which has undertaken the work of exploring how the brain learns and what those findings mean for teachers. "The enormous growth in understanding brain plasticity has created an entirely new way to consider how learning and teaching take place" (Hardiman & Denckla, 2010, p. 4). In these first two chapters, we have offered a brief introduction to these exciting scientific advances. Before we turn next to consider some of the implications of these discoveries for early childhood education, we invite you to continue your exploration of mind, brain, and education research with regular visits to these sites:

- The Dana Foundation (http://www.dana.org) supports and shares brain research with the public.
- The Children's Reading Foundation provides an overview on "Brain Research: Build a Better Brain" (http://www. readingfoundation.org/parents/brain_research.jsp), along with links to developmental milestones for infants, toddlers, and pre-schoolers.
- University of Washington faculty maintain a "Neuroscience for Kids" site (http://faculty.washington.edu/chudler/neurok.html) with links to a video, fun activities, and news articles about the brain.
- The New York Academy of Sciences (http://www.nyas.org) offers an interesting array of articles and podcasts on recent research at its Neuroscience link, under Life Sciences and Biomedical Research.

NOTE

This chapter is adapted with permission from "Ten Key Ideas About the Brain," Chapter 1 of *BrainSMART Early Start: Building the Brain Power of Young Children* (2nd ed.), by Donna Wilson, Lola Heverly, and Marcus Conyers (BrainSMART, 2011).

THREE

Nurturing the Brain and Body

Nutrition and Movement

A newborn begins life with only the most rudimentary abilities to move and communicate, but those capabilities develop quickly. Indeed, the huge gains in development that young children experience in their early years are among the most exciting discoveries in child development research in recent decades. We refer to the way the body and brain work together to accomplish these developmental milestones as the **Body-Brain System**. For infants and young children in particular, body and brain coordination is essential for the acquisition of knowledge and skills. The Body-Brain System is fueled by physical, mental, and emotional health. In this chapter, we explore the role of physical activity and healthy nutrition in fueling the learning of infants and young children. Chapter 4 examines the third component, or how an optimistic outlook and positive emotions support learning gains.

GROWING THROUGH LEARNING IN LEAPS AND BOUNDS

Initially, an infant's movements and sounds are built around needs for nourishment and human interaction. A lusty cry does the trick in notifying an infant's parents that she needs to be fed. By thrusting a fist in her mouth, she may indicate essentially the same thing. When her mother strokes the newborn's cheek, the infant responds with a turn of her head and an open mouth in search of a breast, an innate ability known as the rooting instinct. Not all of her instinctive movements are intended to elicit food, however. Research with rhesus monkeys in the 1960s showed that infants sought physical contact with their mothers to satisfy their needs for affection as well as nourishment (Brooks, 2011). For human infants, contact with parents and other caregivers is soothing and calming and may support emotional and cognitive development (Harmon, 2010). Infants learn from every interaction they have with other people and with their environment; this supports the importance of communicating with them during even mundane tasks like feeding, bathing, and diaper changing (Montanaro, 1991). Movement also communicates less profound needs: By kicking her legs and displaying fussiness, the infant may be trying to indicate that she is too warm or too cold or is experiencing tummy troubles.

The innate movements of the newborn are soon augmented by a progressive acquisition of **postural skills** (the ability to position the body) and **locomotor skills** (the ability to move from place to place). Over the next few months, the child gains the ability to lift her head, to turn from her tummy to her back, and eventually to move from back to tummy. Shortly after that, she is sitting, crawling, pulling herself up, "cruising" along the furniture, standing, and walking—and all of that accomplished within approximately the first year of life. What is most notable about these achievements is their immense predictability. Almost every healthy baby from virtually every part of the world will acquire these skills in essentially the same order and in approximately the same time frame, give or take a few months (Eliot, 1999). The development of these skills takes place during one of the "sensitive periods" of experience-expectant synaptogenesis, discussed in Chapter 1.

Learning to walk is just the beginning for the under-5 set, who are on their way to mastering even more complex movements and physical skills. Soon, they will be running, hopping, skipping, jumping, spinning, throwing, and catching a ball, among a myriad of physical activities. By the time they are 4 or 5 years old, they may get their first taste of competitive sports in a peewee soccer or T-ball league. They may start taking dance or tumbling lessons, discovering the fun of somersaulting and making their first tentative attempts at a cartwheel.

Movement requires physical components such as muscular development and visual acuity. The brain is at work in the development of motor skills, balance, and navigational abilities. The brains of children also equip them with an emerging curiosity to discover what is beyond their immediate surroundings and a desire to test the limits of what their bodies can achieve. Body-brain interconnectivity gives children the ability to move and a sense of direction when they move. From stumbling and falling to coordinating arm and leg movements, children begin to employ their developing ambulatory skills to accomplish a variety of aims. They walk to the toy box in search of toys. They walk and point toward the refrigerator because they know their favorite juice is inside. They run across the yard in play with friends.

Fuel for Learning

Coinciding with children's mastery of physical skills and movement are important changes in their nutritional needs. During the first year of life, a newborn subsists with liquid nourishment from a breast and/or a bottle. By the time the child is 4 to 6 months of age, he begins experiencing a whole new world of solid foods that optimally starts with iron-fortified cereals and pureed fruits and vegetables. From ages 2 to 5, the child is introduced to a wide array of foods and drinks. The most nutritionally beneficial diets will include ample servings of milk, protein, fruits, vegetables, and whole grains.

However, just as children become more physically in control of their movements, they also seek to be more in control of other aspects of their lives, including their diets. Gone are the days of infancy, when children were literally crying for their supper, replaced by the era of toddlerhood, when children are now able to speak and make their preferences known, often in very definitive ways. The battle of wills that may result between adults and children can make mealtime an exhausting experience for everyone involved. A toddler who won't drink his milk or avoids his green beans in favor of a chocolate chip cookie is perhaps setting himself for poor eating habits that last longer than childhood. Green beans for dinner and a cookie with milk for dessert might be a workable compromise. The key for parents and other caregivers is to ensure that the child does not take a pass on the green beans as well as the lean piece of chicken and the whole-grain dinner roll because he stuffed himself with cookies before he ever arrived at the table.

Nutrition and physical movement are two components of a healthy lifestyle that children should learn at an early age. These are among the factors that lead to optimal development of the Body-Brain System. Children are most receptive to learning when healthy bodies and brains work together.

HOW THE BODY AND BRAIN WORK
TOGETHER TO SUPPORT LEARNING

The development of motor skills is a prime example of the Body-Brain System in action. Motor skills involve a lot of feedback, with information going back and forth between the brain and the outside world to accomplish even a simple, single motion. To keep all of the body's movements coordinated and precisely timed, the brain relies on the **cerebellum**, what Eliot (1999) describes as "the air traffic control system of the nervous system" (p. 267). The cerebellum receives input from the motor cortex as well as the various senses and then modifies motor commands to match the intended movement and makes adjustments to ensure that all body movements are proceeding as intended.

Many experts agree that an hour of exercise or physical activity per day, such as running, jumping, swimming, and participating in group activities, is an important component for maintaining body and brain health. A meta-analysis of studies on physical fitness suggests that movement may be especially important to the cognitive development of very young children (Sibley & Etnier, 2003). Sylwester (2010) stresses the central role that physical movement plays in the development and maintenance of a child's brain, citing evidence that formal exercise programs undertaken by schools can have a positive impact on test scores as well as the behavior of students and their physical well-being. The connection between movement and learning is also a foundational element of the Montessori approach to early childhood education; Maria Montessori's classic *The Absorbent Mind* (1967) makes the case that intellectual development is intertwined with physical activity.

Adequate Sleep Energizes Development

Both the body and the brain require adequate sleep for healthy development. Infants need as much as 16 or 17 hours of sleep per 24-hour period, whereas toddlers typically taper off to about 10 to 12 hours, including naps. About half of an infant's sleep time is devoted to rapid-eye-movement (REM) sleep. The quantity of REM sleep in infants, in contrast to adults who engage in less than two hours of REM sleep each night, has led experts to conclude that it is developmentally important (Sylwester, 2010). There is also evidence that sleep in early childhood may play a crucial role in brain development (Frank, Issa, & Stryker, 2001).

Regular sleep cycles are also crucial to development. Monique Le-Bourgeois of Brown University, in studying the effect of sleep on preschoolers, found that the disturbance of the sleep cycle has a profound effect on a child's performance on standardized IQ tests even if the total number of hours spent sleeping is essentially the same (Bronson & Merryman, 2009). Recent research from the American Academy of Sleep Medicine (2009) suggests that sleep quality is just as important as quantity, with students who maintained regular and predictable sleep schedules performing better in school than those who kept irregular schedules and had trouble falling or staying asleep.

The Importance of Good Nutrition

The Body-Brain System works best when fueled by a nutritionally balanced diet. Good nutrition supports a student's ability to learn, whereas poor nutrition or undernourishment can cause children to be more fatigued, less active, and less socially engaged. This is borne out by brain-imaging research that shows a difference in brain wave patterns between undernourished children and their well-fed peers (Barnet & Barnet, 1998).

Parents, caregivers, and early childhood educators should emphasize good nutrition as important for children's physical and neurological well-being. Parents are essentially correct when they tell their children to eat their vegetables because it will help them "grow up big and strong." They could just as easily add "and smarter, too." As researchers have determined, eating nutritious foods is essential not only for young children's bodies but also for their brains. In fact, good nutrition has been correlated with important brain development activity early in a child's life.

Although the brain accounts for only 2% of the body's weight, it uses 20% of the nutrient energy. It is especially important that children consume foods that provide glucose, which is central to neuronal processing, and amino acids, which are vital for neurotransmitter synthesis (Sylwester, 2005). This use of nutrients to fuel learning may be even higher among infants; as noted previously, Meltzoff and colleagues (2009) report that 60% of a newborn's "energy budget" is consumed by the brain.

Glucose comes into the body via nutrients such as complex carbohydrates. Unlike simple carbohydrates, complex carbohydrates are rich in fiber. Whole-grain breads, pastas, and cereals are great examples of complex carbohydrates that, when broken down into glucose, provide energy for the brain as well as the body. Amino acids are represented in our diet by a number of foods, including soybeans, nuts, grains, and the animal proteins in meat, fish, eggs, and dairy products.

A highly sensitive period for brain development occurs from the fifth month of pregnancy to sometime around the child's second birthday. This is a period when synaptic development, dendritic branching, and **myelination** (insulation of neurons to facilitate faster transmission of impulses) are occurring at a rapid rate (see Chapters 1 and 2). In the absence of good nutrition during the mother's pregnancy and the first 2 years of life, children face a danger of severe impairment of their cognitive, emotional, and neurological abilities. Studies have shown that fetuses and young children who are deprived of such nutrition during this **critical period**—in comparison with well-nourished peers of the same culture— were more likely to score poorly on IQ tests, to have problems in school, to lag in language development, and to experience behavioral issues. The good news is that there is evidence that American children in the last several decades have been eating better "brain-building" food—that is, more protein, fresh fruits and vegetables, and vitamin-fortified milk and grains—when compared to children from the early part of the 20th century (Eliot, 1999).

Programs to Make Children "Food-Secure"

A threat to adequate nutrition is **food insecurity**, which refers to limited or uncertain availability of nutritional foods. For families who are coping with food insecurity, help is available through federal, state, and local programs. For example, the U.S. Department of Agriculture administers the Supplemental Nutrition Assistance Program (SNAP), which aims to alleviate poor nutrition in low-income households by making healthy food more accessible to some 46 million participants each month, half of whom are children. Another major governmental program aimed directly at small children is the Special Supplemental Nutrition Program for Women, Infants, and Children (WIC), which provides federal grants to states for supplemental food, nutritional education, and health care referrals to expectant mothers, new mothers, and their children up to the age of 5 at the rate of about 9 million participants per year. A third program that aids in child nutrition is the National School Lunch Program, a federally assisted meal program that provides nutritionally balanced low-cost or free lunches to more than 30 million children on each school day (U.S. Department of Agriculture, 2012b, 2012c, 2012d).

In the last several years, there has been additional focus on improving nutrition among America's children. Such efforts as the Healthy, Hunger-Free Kids Act and First Lady Michelle Obama's Let's Move initiative are targeting the related issues of nutrition and physical health. A key component of these programs is involvement by our nation's schools. In 2011, the USDA announced that more than 1,250 schools had received U.S. School Challenge (HUSSC) honors for expanding nutrition and physical activity opportunities. Schools participating in the program have pledged to provide healthier school lunch menus featuring a wider variety of fruits and vegetables, more frequent use of whole-grain products, and restriction of foods with higher fat, added sugars, and sodium. Additionally, the program focuses on offering nutrition education that teaches children how to make healthier eating choices and on communicating with parents to reinforce those healthier choices at home.

Author Marcus Conyers led a project with a local foundation to coordinate a health improvement program for students of the Orange County (Florida) Public School District (Conyers & Wilson, 2009). Following lessons on nutrition and exercise and efforts to involve and educate parents, students reported healthier eating habits, including eating more vegetables and fruits and reducing sugar intake; increased regular physical activity; and improved hydration during the school day. An analysis found that these changes in eating and exercise habits helped students maintain a healthier weight (Wang & Ellis, 2005); teachers also reported measurable academic gains, decreased absenteeism, and improved classroom management (Watson, 2010).

DEVELOPING HEALTHY EATING HABITS

You are what you eat, but in many cases, babies and toddlers are what their parents eat. Children learn from example. If parents are eating healthy, nutritious foods, this sets the stage (or, more precisely, the table) for their children to do the same thing. As parents cook and serve meals to their children, they, when possible, should offer healthy selections that can instill good eating habits for a lifetime. As an example, consider the simple but important choice of offering whole-grain foods instead of processed grains. The USDA recommends that at least half the grains in your diet be whole. In other words, whole-wheat bread should trump white bread, oatmeal is preferable to cornflakes, and whole-wheat pasta is better than regular spaghetti.

Other habits can be likewise enforced if parents, caregivers, and early childhood programs are conscientious in the selections they make for children. Start them off with a healthy breakfast to support a day focused on healthy development (oatmeal with sliced bananas and milk is a good choice). Serve 100% apple juice instead of sugary substitutes. Offer raisins or apple slices for lunch instead of potato chips, and make that peanut butter sandwich on whole-wheat bread. Load dinner plates with plenty of vegetables along with a serving of protein (for example, meat or fish). Children should be eating four or five servings of fruits and vegetables each day—and the more colorful these selections are, the better. Make sure the food choices you provide are high in vitamins and minerals. Iron and calcium are especially important nutrients for growing children.

Keep in mind that a child's growing body and brain are different from those of an adult. One such difference is the fat content that a child—especially a young one—needs to have present in his diet. In the critical brain development stage before the age of 2, children should be eating a diet that is rich in fat with such choices as milk, yogurt, cheese, and meat (Perlmutter & Colman, 2006).

Another key to peak body-brain efficiency is water. The brain is an electrical and chemical system that needs water to transmit information efficiently. Children should drink plenty of water on a daily basis and steer clear of beverages that are high in sugar and/or fat content that could cause dehydration and be a deterrent to effective learning.

THE MORE THEY PLAY, THE MORE THEY LEARN

Adequate sleep and nutrition give young children the energy they need to pursue one of their favorite activities: play. It's hard to overstate the importance of free play and more directed "playful learning" to support the development of young children's language, problem-solving, social, and creative abilities (Hirsh-Pasek, Golinkoff, Berk, & Singer, 2009). Throughout this text, we return again and again to the opportunities for children to learn through play.

Children play with various toys that teach them how to sort objects by shape or color, how to stack, how to count, how to say the letters of the alphabet, and how wheeled objects can go from point A to point B. When playing with others, they learn the concepts of sharing or taking turns (though not always willingly, at first). As they grow older, they learn such concepts as problem solving and perseverance. A determined 4-year-old may get discouraged when her block tower keeps falling down, but she doesn't give up, figures out a better way to build it, and the sixth time she tries—success! Thus, play provides many paths to mastery, a topic we will discuss in more depth in Chapter 4.

Play is common among all mammals, but as Frost (1998) noted, human infants are reliant on their parents to give structure and direction to play due to their motor immaturity during the first few months of life. However, as neural development proceeds, the range and complexity of play increases quickly. Play has a significant role in healthy development, with evidence that it facilitates linkages of language, emotion, movement, socialization, and cognition (CERI, 2007).

There are several different types of play. *Object play* involves interacting with toys (or the spoons and pots from the kitchen cupboards). *Locomotor play* is characterized by such activities as running, jumping, and playing tag. The most sophisticated form of play is **social play**, which often involves pretending and most often occurs among animals—humans included—that exhibit a strong amount of behavioral flexibility and plasticity (Aamodt & Wang, 2011). Playing "house" or collectively jumping inside a big cardboard box and pretending it's a spaceship headed for Mars are forms of social play. Author Donna Wilson remembers that pretend play of "being the teacher" and helping other children learn how to read was one of her favorite things to do—even before she began school and learned to comprehend sentences on the page!

Active Play as a Path to Healthy Development

Another benefit of play for young children especially relevant to the development of the Body-Brain System is that it increases their competence in basic motor skills, continuing the developmental process that began in infancy. "The mastery of most motor skills requires considerable practice, which must be in the form of sufficiently pleasant experiences for the child to continue doing them" (Sylwester, 2010, p. 29). Motor skill development encompasses locomotor abilities, object control (throwing, catching, and kicking), stability, coordination, and balance. Research indicates that more vigorous physical activity may be more effective in improving motor skills than light activity; young children who spend the most time in rigorous play (i.e., running, skipping, and climbing that increases their heart and respiratory rates) had better motor skills than their less active peers (Shenouda, Gabel, & Timmons, 2011).

Encouraging and leading young children in active play may well pay lifelong dividends. Citing worldwide trends in childhood and adult obesity, a group of Canadian researchers (Timmons, Proudfoot, MacDonald, Bray, & Cairney, 2012) has begun a major study on the relationship between physical activity and health outcomes for preschoolers. Just as we advocate for the early development of cognitive skills to support future success in school and in life, we believe that guiding young children to develop healthy eating and exercise habits early may set them on the right path to maintain those habits as adolescents and adults. In addition, active play by young children may contribute to cognitive development, socialization, and improved attention to learning tasks (Murray & Fortinberry, 2006).

Transitioning from Play to Other Activities

Because play is pleasurable, children can engage in it for hours—and you might actually have a hard time getting them to move on to other activities. This is both a good thing—because it keeps children motivated to continue what is presumably a positive learning experience—and a bad thing—because it makes it extremely hard for a parent or an educator to impress upon children that it's time to do something else. How many parents are frustrated in trying to enforce bedtime because their children plead for more time with their favorite toys? How many educators have had trouble bringing their young charges back into the classroom when interrupting a lively session of tag on the playground? For parents, one option might be to allow time for a bedtime snack of graham crackers and milk followed by reading a favorite storybook, then segueing more quietly into bedtime. Educators might read a favorite story and let children act out the parts to help ease the transition of moving on to another activity.

ATTENTION! MAINTAINING FOCUS THROUGH PHYSICAL ACTIVITY AND VARIETY

While children benefit from the unfettered experience of play, a key component of learning is capturing and maintaining **attention**. Attention is the ability to **focus** on a specific object, task, or piece of information without being distracted by extraneous stimuli. It is dependent on the individual's interest in and comprehension of the task or subject at hand. If a child finds something boring or hard to understand, attention is harder to hold. Attention also depends on the child's alertness and physical comfort. A sleep-deprived child, or one who is hungry or overheated, is not as attentive as a child who is well rested, well fed, and listening to a teacher in a well-ventilated room.

Taking distractions out of the environment is also an important component of attention. It is difficult for a parent to have a serious discussion with a child when the child's favorite television show is blaring in the background. Similarly, it is difficult for a teacher to command the full attention of a room full of children when laughter from another room is echoing down the hallway. It's better to close the door than to let children wonder: "What are they doing in there that is so much more fun than what we're doing in here?" By shutting out the distractions, the teacher stands a far better chance of creating her own engrossing educational experience that commands the attention as well as the enjoyment of the children in her room.

Setting aside time for physical activity is another effective way to help children improve their attention. Exercise not only burns off surplus energy but also helps children become refreshed and better able to focus on their thinking and learning tasks (Wilson & Conyers, 2011b). There are documented instances of formal exercise programs in school leading to higher test scores as well as improved behavior among students (Sylwester, 2010). In addition, a study of more than 200 school-age children in Italy concluded that the students had higher levels of attention after they partook of physical education classes, with the physiological arousal that accompanies exercise identified as the cause of enhanced attention to lesson content and activities (Gallotta et al., 2012).

Bottom-Up vs. Top-Down

It is helpful to distinguish between two forms of attention systems: **bottom-up,** which is activated by the stimuli around you, and **top-down,** which is the deliberate focus of your brain on a specific task (Aamodt & Wang, 2011). The bottom-up system gains attention through the blare of a police siren, the ring of a telephone, the smell of unattended food burning in the oven—any number of events that cause an immediate reaction and often a distraction from whatever it was that we were previously doing. The top-down system, meanwhile, is directed by the brain's cortex to focus voluntarily on a task such as homework or preparing a gourmet meal.

Often, the attention that is directed by the top-down system is immediately drawn away by the bottom-up system. While the bottom-up system is functional at birth, the top-down system takes time to develop and improves throughout the life span. This explains why younger children are more easily distracted than older children and why it is more difficult to retain their attention.

Accounting for the Attention Cycle

Because of the younger child's propensity for distraction, it's advisable for early childhood educators to plan the duration of activities with this in mind. A good rule of thumb is to plan 2 to 5 minutes of focus for each year of age. Thus, the optimal time for a 3-year-old to be engaged in an activity is 6 to 15 minutes. Even in that short period, the child's brain is likely to shift in and out of high attention. For that reason, it is more appropriate to talk about an **attention cycle** rather than an attention span (Wilson et al., 2011). The highest level of attention in this cycle is typically at the beginning and end—referred to as **primacy** and **recency**, respectively. It is therefore most effective to organize learning in chunks of time that are appropriate to the child's age and to present the most important information first and last, when attention is at its greatest.

Working against the ability to provide attention is the state of **neuronal habituation. Habituation** is characterized by monotony—giving the brain too much of one signal, such as one sound (monotone) or one voice (monologue)—thus causing a child to tune out and be more prone to distractions. Habituation is a strong force, even during infancy. The key to combating habituation is to provide variety—for instance, by adding new toys or rotating existing toys in and out of the child's play areas and by offering diverse experiences, such as walks to the park, trips to the zoo or library, or visits to other people's homes. This is not only effective in improving a child's attention but is also beneficial in providing the stimulation required for brain development (Eliot, 1999).

LEARNING HOW TO LEARN

Selective Attention

As we noted in Chapter 1, young children can begin to develop cognitive strategies to take charge of their learning and become "the boss of their brains." By introducing these ideas in simple terms, you can guide children to understand thinking and learning as processes they can control and master.

In this era of information overload and multitasking, we can all benefit from improving our selective attention. The concept of paying attention may be beyond the understanding of very young children, but 4- and 5-year-olds should be able to grasp this idea. The story of Lazeen the Focused Eagle (see Textbox 3.1) introduces the skill of focusing one's attention. Before sharing this story, you might want to introduce the key words *focus* and *attention* so children will be listening to discover how Lazeen uses the problem-solving skill of selective attention.

Textbox 3.1. Learn With Us

The Story of Lazeen the Focused Eagle

Message: By focusing on an important mission, an eagle does a good deed for her friend.
Key words to introduce: *focus, attention*

Lazeen the eagle loved to fly high in the clear blue sky. She could look down and see the trees and the river and the little village where her human friend Jasmine lived. She could see the park where Jasmine played, with its swings and monkey bars and see-saws.

One day, Jasmine lost her ring while she was playing in the park. "Oh, no!" Jasmine said. "My grandma gave me that ring. She said it would always bring me luck."

From up in the sky, Lazeen saw Jasmine waving at her. The eagle landed on her favorite tree next to Jasmine. She could see that Jasmine was very sad.

"Lazeen," Jasmine cried, "please help me find my ring. I lost it somewhere in the park. I know you can see everything from up there in the sky. Can you see my ring?"

Lazeen took flight and circled around the park. There was so much to see! She saw children playing on the swings and playing tag from tree to tree and flying kites. There was so much to see that Lazeen forgot to look for the ring.

When she landed, Jasmine came running up to her favorite tree. "Did you find it?" Jasmine asked. "Did you find my ring?"

Lazeen took flight again, and this time she did not look at the children on the swings or playing tag or flying kites. But there were other children throwing a big red ball into the air and catching when it fell. Lazeen swooped down near the ball and made the children laugh.

When Lazeen landed on her tree again, Jasmine said, "Did you find my ring? Was it by the children with the big red ball?"

"Oh, no," Lazeen thought. "I forgot about the ring *again*. This time, I will focus only on finding Jasmine's ring."

This time as the eagle flew over the park, she did not look at the children on the swings or playing tag or flying kites or tossing the big red ball. She focused only on looking for the ring. She flew in a circle around the park until she saw a shiny thing in the grass. Lazeen swooped down, opened her beak, and snagged the ring!

As Lazeen settled onto her favorite tree, she opened her beak and the ring dropped into Jasmine's hand. "Oh, you found it!" Jasmine said happily. "I knew you could do it."

"Yes," thought Lazeen, "all I had to do was focus and pay attention!"

Activity: Introduce Concentration-style card games that require staying focused and paying attention.

These stories are adapted with permission from the *Thinking for Reading Curriculum,* by Donna Wilson and Marcus Conyers (BrainSMART, 2005).

MOVEMENT, MUSIC, AND MEMORY

Another set of cognitive skills young children can begin to develop involves memory strategies, particularly those that combine movement and music. Physical activity when set to music is particularly helpful as a memory aid by using the power of rhythm and repetition. Music activates the temporal lobe, which is involved in hearing and memory. Listening to music is evocative, both in terms of the emotions it elicits and the strong memories it brings forth. Consider, for instance, the theme from *Jaws*. Movie audiences in the 1970s felt a sense of foreboding as soon as the sound of John Williams's composition filled the theater. Decades later, just the first few notes from the movie soundtrack have the power to bring forth the image of an enormous man-eating shark. The "da-dum, da-dum" theme has also enshrined itself in our pop culture as a way to deliver mildly unpleasant news in a mock-serious way.

Music perception begins shortly after birth, with musical aptitude continuing to develop throughout the first decade of a child's life (Aamodt & Wang, 2010). In Chapter 1, we described how newborns respond to motherese, the high-pitched melodious form of speaking that engages and comforts them. A study shows that 4-month-old babies prefer the exaggerated **prosody** of motherese to other forms of speech (Fernald, 1985). Prosody refers to the rhythm and speech intonations of language, which in motherese has a music-like quality. Parents and other caregivers instinctively use motherese around newborns, and many adults are equally inclined to sing lullabies or nursery rhymes to infants as well. Babies tend to enjoy this musical interaction, as evidenced by a study that showed greater responsiveness among 6-month-olds when their mothers sang to them as opposed to when their mothers merely spoke to them (Nakata & Trehub, 2004).

The way that music engages even young children provides a plausible explanation for why we tend to remember words more easily when they are set to music. Decades may have passed since you last heard the theme song from your favorite cartoon show, but if asked to sing it, you would likely be able to recall every word. Contrast that with how well you can remember facts from a high school algebra or civics class. Had those classes been set to music, you might better be able to recall them, too.

Because of their rhythm and rhyming schemes, songs can be effective **mnemonic** devices that aid children in learning. The undisputed cham-

Table 3.1. AEIOU in Action: Music and Memory

A	Awareness	The children have been learning about colors in different play activities, so when a cardinal lands on the bird feeder, one child announces, "Look! A red bird!" The teacher supplies the name *cardinal*.
E	Exploration	Together, the teacher and children decide to see how many different colors of birds they can spot. Soon, they spot a robin with an orange breast and a finch with yellow wings.
I	Inquiry	The teacher asks, "How can we remember which birds have red feathers and which are orange and yellow?" One child suggests, "We can make a song like our color song!" They all think for a moment, and then the teacher sings, "There's a robin, there's a cardinal" to the familiar tune of *Frere Jacques*.
O	Order	Another child calls out, "Don't forget the finch!" Then they put the colors of the birds in the same order to complete their song: "There's a robin. There's a cardinal. There's a finch, there's a finch! Orange and red and yellow . . ." "We need a word that rhymes with yellow," the teacher suggests. They come up with *jello*, *hello*, and *fellow* before agreeing on the final lines: ". . . Sing a happy hello! In the trees. In the trees."
U	Understanding/ Use	The next day the children run to the edge of the playground singing their new song. They spot an orange-breasted robin and a yellow finch, and then one child spots a blue jay. "Blue!" he calls. "We have to make our song bigger!"

pion of musical mnemonics is "The ABC Song," which toddlers learn to sing long before they even know what an alphabet is for. There are also educational songs that teach children the 50 states and the order of the planets (though Pluto's demotion, alas, has caused a change of lyrics). Dickinson (2001b) recommends that teachers introduce children to potentially unfamiliar words in lyrics and discuss their meaning so that children may hear them as distinct words rather than getting confused with syllables and sounds linked to rhythm, tune, and phrasing.

Action songs that couple music with movement are especially effective in engaging young children. When an adult teaches an action song to young children, they see the movement, follow the movement (bringing into play mirror neurons), hear the music, and sing the song. Even simple actions songs like "I'm a Little Teapot" or "London Bridge" are fun and invigorating for young children who are still in the process of mastering basic verbal and motor skills. They involve several of the forms of intelligence identified in Chapter 2, including mathematic/logical, verbal/linguistic, musical/rhythmic, bodily/kinesthetic, and (when performed in groups) interpersonal. There also is evidence that musical instrument lessons enhance spatial-temporal reasoning. In a study of preschoolers, for instance, it was determined that musical keyboard training improved young children's ability to perform spatial-temporal tasks in comparison to various control groups (Rauscher et al., 1997).

Memory experts make a distinction between **explicit memories**, which are tied to specific experiences, and **implicit memories**, which are the skills and knowledge that we pick up even though we often don't remember the experience of learning them (Eliot, 1999). Children learn their ABCs and nursery rhymes through song-aided memory devices that they will remember forever, but they may not remember the specific experience of singing these songs with their parents or their preschool class.

Nonetheless, early childhood educators and parents can take pride in the fact that, while many specific experiences from the under-5-year-old's life will not likely be remembered in adulthood, the skills and knowledge taught to them today lay a foundation for further learning that will last a lifetime.

Chapter 1 introduced the AEIOU cycle of learning through awareness, exploration, inquiry, order, and understanding and use. In Table 3.1, we apply this cycle to music and memory with an example of a group of 4-year-olds watching birds in the trees near their playground.

☆*PRACTICAL TIPS FOR EARLY CHILDHOOD EDUCATORS*☆

Nurturing the Body-Brain System

Look for opportunities every day to teach young children the importance of a healthy body and a healthy brain.

Focus on eating healthy. The USDA's new food guidance system, Choose My Plate, uses a colorful graphic to explain the importance of a well-balanced diet of protein, grains, fruits, vegetables, and dairy (http://www.choosemyfood.gov). Displaying the Choose My

Plate poster in your room is an excellent way to emphasize the benefits of good nutritional habits. Here are some other ideas:

- Start a conversation about healthy foods. Ask children: "What are your favorite foods?" Provide positive feedback when they mention fruits, vegetables, and other healthy choices.
- Introduce children to food labels and explain the various benefits of iron, calcium, and other vitamins and minerals listed.
- Reinforce your conversations by providing coloring pages of healthy foods. If you have a play kitchen, make sure you have fruits, vegetables, and milk bottles represented among your plastic fare.
- Share stories that underscore the importance of healthy eating, and point out to children when a character is being a good eater. If kids are reluctant to try new foods, you might want to read Dr. Seuss's *Green Eggs and Ham*, a classic example of a character who had no idea how good green food tasted until he tried it.
- For special occasions and holiday parties, request that parents bring healthy foods, such as fruit salad, veggies and yogurt dip, and fruit juice instead of sugary drinks. A nutritious idea from the USDA's Center for Nutrition Policy and Promotion is to ask families to bring in ingredients to make a homemade trail mix. Use a variety of nuts, dried fruits, and whole-grain cereals to create a nutritious snack that will taste just as good or better than a premade trail mix.

Build in regular physical exercise and movement. Learning is best achieved when children are given the opportunity to stand, stretch, run, and play. Time in the playground for informal, unstructured play is important for young children who still have limited capacity for attention. To involve their bodies in their daily educational routine, you may choose to do the following:

- Indulge their enjoyment of music and movement by playing a recording of favorite children's songs, such as "The Wheels on the Bus" or "Head, Shoulders, Knees, and Toes." Have children get up on their feet, get in a circle, and do the movements together.
- Play "animal charades." Have children take turns acting out their favorite animals and let the other kids guess what animal

they are supposed to be. Play a game of musical chairs using your recording of children's songs. Or try another favorite: Duck, Duck, Goose.

- Young children also need downtime to rest and rejuvenate. Plan a routine that works well around daily naps or quiet time.

Let children participate in the "work" of play. Chapter 1 offers several tips on keeping play engaging for young children. Avoiding the problem of habituation means providing variety in both playthings and activities. While one of the primary reasons to play is to have fun, there are several ways to make play a worthwhile learning experience as well:

- Build opportunities for sharing and taking turns into the play experience. Monitor the play activity to ensure that both assertive and less-assertive children are getting an equal amount of playtime. Reiterate the concept of sharing for those who are having trouble relinquishing a toy or recognizing when their turn has ended.
- Encourage children's creativity when they use playthings in unusual ways. Who's to say that a rectangular block can't be used as a telephone or that the toy telephone can't be the instrument panel of a rocket ship?
- Make sure the toys and games you provide are age-appropriate. Puzzles that are too easy or too hard will not hold the interest of a toddler or preschooler for very long. Toys are especially valuable if they have an intrinsic reward ("I finished the puzzle," "I won the game," "I built the tower") that provides children with a sense of accomplishment and a willingness to continue to engage in play as a positive and constructive activity.

Look for opportunities to underscore that children are the boss of their brains. This chapter introduced two cognitive skills that will help children become better prepared to "do school": selective attention and strategies to enhance memory. Emphasize that these are learnable, useful skills just like learning to recognize letters or button your coat:

- "Thank you, everyone, for paying attention to our special visitor today!"

- "You remembered all the words to our weather song. That's great!"
- "Let's all pay attention to Sabrina now. It is her turn to share."

FOUR

Cultivating Optimism

How Positive Emotions Support Learning

Beyond promoting physical health through good nutrition and regular physical activity, parents and early childhood educators can help young children optimize their Body-Brain Systems for learning by guiding them to develop an optimistic outlook. This emphasis on emotional health can help children become more resilient and likely to persist in learning tasks until they succeed, especially when they have the support of parents and educators who believe in their learning potential. In this chapter, we explore why both children and adults should strive to develop a positive approach—and how to do so.

The traditional view that thinking and feeling are separate functions— that learning is an intellectual process entirely detached from emotions— has been largely discounted by neuroscientific research in recent decades:

> Emotion works with cognition in an integrated and seamless way to enable us to navigate the world of relationships, work, and spiritual growth. When positive emotion energizes us, we are better able to concentrate, to figure out the social networks at a new job or new school, to broaden our thinking so we can creatively integrate diverse information, and to sustain our interest in a task so we can persevere. . . . A *feeling* permeates virtually everything we do. No wonder then, that circuits in the brain that control and regulate emotions overlap with those involved in functions we think as purely cognitive. (Davidson, 2012, p. 89)

In other words, the work of educators to guide children to become "the boss of their brains" involves taking charge of both thinking and feeling.

IMPACT ON CHILDREN'S LEARNING

Educational research shows that how children think about their ability to make learning gains can have a significant impact on their academic performance. Dweck's (2006) studies on "mindsets" and motivation indicate that when students believe they can get smarter, they are more likely to persist in the hard work needed for incremental learning, or making progressive improvement in skills and knowledge. On the other hand, children and adolescents who believe that their intelligence is fixed—that no amount of effort and learning will make them smarter—are less motivated to persist in their studies. The classic story of the Little Engine That Could is a brilliant example of these findings on a level that young children can understand: The little blue engine huffed and puffed "I think I can! I think I can!" and kept chugging away up the mountain pass until she made it up and over. In the same way, children who believe they can learn new things are more likely to put in the work required to do so.

Of course, early childhood educators and parents know that many young children naturally have what Dweck describes as a "growth mindset": They have big dreams and beliefs in their abilities to accomplish them. But at some point in their lives, some children begin to rein in their aspirations about what they can achieve. They may be influenced by subtle but pervasive cultural messages that only a chosen few have the special talents required to succeed. Expectations from parents and teachers also help to shape children's beliefs in their potential to reach their goals.

The term **Pygmalion effect** refers to the influence that expectations can have on student achievement. This term derives from a classroom study in the 1960s in which teachers were told that certain students scored extremely high on aptitude tests and could be expected to do very well academically that year. The teachers were told not to single those students out for specialized instruction or treatment. By the end of the school year, the identified students had indeed made great progress—even though their test scores nine months previously had actually been just average. In discussing that research, Achor (2010) notes that when teachers expected their students to make significant academic gains, "the belief the teachers had in the students' potential had been unwittingly and nonverbally communicated. More important, these nonverbal messages were then digested by the students and transformed into reality" (p. 84). Similarly, Hattie (2009) reports on studies showing that parents' high hopes and expectations for their students' academic performance are closely correlated with achievement.

Unfortunately, the opposite is also true: Students' performance too often conforms to adults' low expectations. In his 2009 examination of more than 800 meta-analyses on teaching and learning, Hattie found many studies indicating that teachers' expectations for students based on socioeconomic, racial, and ethnic status, gender, or labels of gifted or disabled learners may have an impact on performance; furthermore, "students know they are treated differentially in the classroom due to expectations by teachers, and are quite accurate in informing on how teachers differ in the degree to which they favor some children over others with higher expectations" (p. 124).

Optimism and other positive traits can be uncannily predictive of academic success. Tough (2012) recounts the experience of a highly lauded eighth-grade class at KIPP Academy Middle School in the South Bronx during the late 1990s. The students, all minorities and almost all from low-income families, were finishing up four years at KIPP (an acronym for "Knowledge Is Power Program"), an ambitious educational experiment with the goal of supporting students to become top scholastic performers. The class gained widespread media acclaim for earning the highest test scores of any school in the Bronx and ranking near the top for the whole of New York City. However, a long-term measurement of success for the program was dependent on how well the students did in high school and college after leaving KIPP. Those results were disappointing, with just eight students, 21% of the class, earning their four-year college degrees. What was surprising, however, was that the students who completed college were not those who did the best academically at KIPP, as Tough explained:

> Instead, they seemed to be the ones who possessed certain other gifts, skills like optimism and resilience, and social agility. They were the students who were able to recover from bad grades and resolve to do better next time; who could bounce back from unhappy breakups or fights with their parents; who could persuade professors to give them

extra help after class; who could resist the urge to go out to the movies and instead stay home and study. . . . For young people without the benefit of a lot of family resources, without the kind of safety net that their wealthier peers enjoyed, these characteristics proved to be an indispensable part of making it to college graduation day. (p. 52)

In other words, an optimistic, can-do attitude fuels the persistence and resilience needed to accomplish ambitious academic goals.

WHAT OPTIMISM IS—AND ISN'T

To help children overcome societal messages that they may not have what it takes to pursue their dreams, one powerful antidote may be to guide them to develop an optimistic outlook. In their book *The Optimistic Child* (2007), Seligman, Reivich, Jaycox, and Gillham note that many parents share common goals for their children:

We want our children to have lives filled with friendship and love and high deeds. We want them to be eager to learn and be willing to confront challenges. We want our children to be grateful for what they receive from us, but to be proud of their own accomplishments. We want them to grow up with confidence in the future, a love of adventure, a sense of justice, and courage enough to act on that sense of justice. We want them to be resilient in the face of the setbacks and failures that growing up always brings. And when the time comes, we want them to be good parents. Our fondest hope is that the quality of their lives will be better than our own, and our inmost prayer is that our children will have all of our strengths and few of our weaknesses. (p. 6)

A pervasive obstacle to realizing those hopes for children is what the authors call "an epidemic of pessimism," readily evident in the high incidence of depression in the United States and depictions of violence and despair children might be exposed to in movies, television, and other media. Children may also be coping with problems beyond their control in their homes and neighborhoods. There is a genetic component to developing a pessimistic outlook, and environmental factors may also contribute to developing this attitude, such as pessimism exhibited by parents and other influential adults and experiences conveying that children have little control over their lives and their futures.

However, practitioners from the field of positive psychology (e.g., Murray & Fortinberry, 2006; Seligman et al., 2007; Seligman, 2011) maintain that children can be taught the power of optimism and that an optimistic outlook can make a difference in their lives. Seligman and colleagues (2007) suggest that optimism is not "chanting happy thoughts to yourself" (p. 297). The degree to which we exhibit optimism or pessimism is represented in our responses to adversity—our beliefs about the consequences when something goes wrong— as demonstrated by three questions:

- Is it personal?
- Is it pervasive?
- Is it permanent?

In this view of these two outlooks, pessimists tend to take setbacks personally ("It's all my fault!") and see problems as pervasive and permanent ("This is going to ruin my life—forever!"). Optimists, on the other hand, don't heap all the blame on themselves, and they tend to see setbacks as limited in scope and temporary.

We can guide children—and ourselves—to adopt this more positive outlook, and there is good reason to do so: Optimists live longer on average than their pessimistic peers, and they tend to be healthier and more successful and experience greater enjoyment of life. A body of educational research (see, for example, Gilman, Huebner, and Furlong's 2009 book *Handbook of Positive Psychology in Schools*) indicates that optimism and other positive characteristics may be predictive of high academic achievement, health, happiness, and career success. Equally important is the finding that optimism can be taught and learned. That is why we place such an emphasis on teaching and modeling an optimistic approach with young children. Writing for parents, Seligman and colleagues (2007) observe that

> when you teach your child optimism, you are teaching him to know himself, to be curious about his theory of himself and of the world. You are teaching him to take an active stance in his world and to shape his own life, rather than be a passive recipient of what happens his way. (p. 297)

LEARNING HOW TO LEARN

Practical Optimism

A powerful way to guide children to realize their potential is to foster a positive learning environment in which every child feels safe, secure, valued, and encouraged to take intellectual risks (Wilson & Conyers,

2011a). When children are positive and happy, their Body-Brain Systems work more efficiently. They are more creative. They solve problems more effectively. They are more engaged in learning and in interacting in positive ways with their peers. Positive relationships with their teachers and caregivers set the tone for an optimal learning environment. When children feel accepted and valued, they respond in kind to their teacher and other children. In our approach to helping educators increase learning, a central message is the need to stay positive and to empower children to do the same. An optimistic, can-do attitude helps children stay energized, on task, and motivated.

We also advocate for explicit instruction on the cognitive asset of **practical optimism**, which may be defined as an approach to life that focuses on taking practical positive action to increase the probability of successful outcomes (Wilson & Conyers, 2011b). The major advantage of developing practical optimism is a boost in persistence in achieving what you set out to do. People with an optimistic outlook are more likely to be undaunted by setbacks and challenges and to keep trying until they succeed. Their perseverance is fueled by their beliefs that they will prevail over adversity, learn from their failures, and overcome plateaus in performance and progress. On the other hand, pessimists are more likely to give up, drop out, and doubt their abilities. Where pessimists see obstacles as a reason to quit, optimists see one more task to complete, one more puzzle to solve on the road to success. The story of Brightside the Optimistic Puppy, featured in Textbox 4.1, exemplifies this can-do spirit for young children.

Textbox 4.1. Learn With Us

The Story of Brightside, the Optimistic Puppy

Message: Children (and puppies!) who are optimistic about their abilities to learn and succeed are more likely to do so.
Key words to introduce: optimism, succeed

Brightside is a happy puppy.

When it rains, the other puppies are sad. But Brightside says, "I love puddles!"

When it is time to go inside after playtime, the other puppies are sad. But Brightside says, "I love cuddling up next to the fire!"

When it is bath time, the other puppies are sad. But Brightside says, "I love bubbles!"

His mama calls him "my little optimist." Brightside doesn't know what that means, but it makes him happy just to hear her say it!

Brightside has many favorite things. His most favorite thing is playing with his boy Jack. The puppy loves to go for walks with Jack and learn new things. He learns how to shake his paw. He learns how to bark when Jack gives him a signal. He learns how to balance a treat on his nose. Brightside doesn't always learn new things on the first try, but he knows that if he keeps trying, he will succeed.

One day, Jack decides to teach Brightside how to catch a ball. "Oh, boy!" Brightside thinks. "A new favorite thing!"

Jack throws the ball. Brightside runs fast and far. He runs so fast and so far the ball falls behind him. "Great!" Brightside thinks. "Now I know not to run so fast and so far."

Jack throws the ball again. This time Brightside runs slower and not so far. The ball sails over his head. "Great!" Brightside thinks. "Now I know not to run too fast or too slow. If I watch the ball carefully, this time I'll catch it."

Jack throws the ball one more time. Brightside watches the ball fly through the sky, and he runs toward it at just the right speed. Then he jumps up and catches it!

"Yay!" Jack calls. "I knew you could do it."

"Yay!" Brightside barks. "I knew I could do it, too! All I had to do was keep learning and trying! I love catching balls!"

Activity: Invite children to share something important they have recently learned how to do.

These stories are adapted with permission from the *Thinking for Reading Curriculum*, by Donna Wilson and Marcus Conyers (BrainSMART, 2005).

THE POWER OF "LOOK WHAT I CAN DO!"

In addition to direct discussions about maintaining a positive approach to learning, persisting through setbacks, and interacting in a positive way with others, you can help children develop and maintain an optimistic outlook by giving them an opportunity to achieve *mastery* of new knowledge and skills. As Seligman and colleagues (2007) define this term, mastery permits young children to take control of a task and affect the outcome through their actions. For infants, opportunities for mastery arise when they play with toys that make sounds as they press buttons or pull levers, for example, or when an adult mimics their actions such as clapping or banging a spoon on the table. In other words, these responses are contingent on children's actions.

Incremental learning and choice may support children to achieve feelings of mastery (Seligman et al., 2007). *Incremental learning* refers to guiding children to undertake relatively complex challenges or new experiences in small, achievable steps, beginning at a level within their control and progressing steadily. This step-by-step approach allows children to have small successes along the way so that they are more likely to persevere if and when they encounter setbacks. Giving children reasonable choices—which book to read, which toys to play with or centers to play in, which snacks to eat—enhances their feelings of being in control.

Many opportunities for mastery arise during the day: during playtime, at meals, when getting dressed to outside to explore. Playtime and guided playful learning offer many such instances: "Play builds cognitive knowledge by offering countless opportunities for sustained attention, problem solving, symbolic representation (e.g., the banana as a phone), memory development, and hypothesis testing" (Hirsh-Pasek et al., 2009, p. 36).

Along the way to gaining mastery, children will experience some setbacks and failures. These are stepping stones to learning advances—as long as adults resist the urge to intervene and solve the problems themselves or to criticize or correct possible solutions as children formulate them, try them out, and refine them (Seligman et al., 2007). One thing teachers and parents can do is model problem solving by "thinking aloud" about how best to address and overcome their own setbacks. For example, "oh, no, our computer isn't working right now, and I was going to find some information about animals. I wonder where else I might look to find what I need?"

Murray and Fortinberry (2006) offer "five principles of HAPPY parenting" that may also have applications in the early childhood classroom for supporting children toward learning successes:

Table 4.1. AEIOU in Action: Practical Optimism

A	Awareness	Using sidewalk chalk, a 3-year-old is working hard to draw stars that look like the celestial bodies in the space mural hanging on the wall of her preschool. But she is becoming more and more frustrated. "Draw a star for me!" she demands of her teacher. The teacher responds, "Oh, stars can be hard—with all those points! I bet if you keep trying, you will draw a star."
E	Exploration	The teacher reminds the girl of the story they read yesterday about Brightside the puppy and how he learned to catch a ball because he kept trying and trying.
I	Inquiry	The girl runs to the mural to get a closer look. She sees stars of many shapes and sizes. Some have more points than others. Some are yellow, but some seem to be pink and blue. She returns to the blacktop and draws a small yellow circle and then adds a few lines around the outside to serve as points.
O	Order	The child next selects light blue chalk and draws a larger star. And then a pink one and a green one—all of different sizes and with different designs of points. Her friend stops and asks, "What are you doing?" "Making stars!" the girl says, pointing to the mural. Soon her friend and other children have joined in, and the blacktop is covered with stars and moons and planets.
U	Understanding/ Use	"Look what you've done!" the teacher tells her happily. "You have your own Milky Way here! I love all the different colors and sizes." The little girl smiles and says, "I can make all sorts of stars!"

- Have a go, or encourage children to take a chance on something new.
- Accept both success and failure by reframing setbacks as opportunities to try again or to try another tack.
- Practice. The authors use the example of guiding infants to learn to walk by providing a safe environment where they have opportunities to pull themselves up, balance along tables and chairs, fall down safely, and get back up and try again. Toddlers need chances to experiment if something doesn't go right the first time. Adults can model the benefits of perseverance by trying a tough task two or three times before they get it right.
- Plan for the best outcome. Involving children in planning helps them understand that some rewards are not immediate, which is a key aspect of self-regulation (see Chapter 6).

- Yes! Make optimism and a confident attitude a habit by celebrating successes.

In Table 4.1, we apply the AEIOU learning cycle to helping children develop their practical optimism.

LEARNING TOGETHER IN PLAY

Maintaining positive relationships and interactions with their peers supports children's sense of optimism and well-being in early childhood programs—and later in school and in life. Much of the value of playtime and guided playful learning activities comes from learning social interactions, such as how to share, take turns, negotiate, and collaborate. Play also allows children to explore a wide variety of challenges and potential solutions that prepare them for more consequential challenges they may face in the future (Sylwester, 2010).

Social learning through play and playful learning improves interpersonal skills that will help young children be ready to "do school" and enhances language skills as well. Hirsh-Pasek and colleagues cite studies showing that "the amount of time 3-year-olds spent talking with peers while pretending was positively associated with the size of their vocabulary two years later after they had begun kindergarten"; another study found "clear and consistent relationships between children's talk during play and their later literacy outcomes" (2009, p. 30). Or, as Katz (2001) puts it, "language is fundamental to the process of learning and engaging in social pretend play" (p. 59).

Engaging With Educators

Karen Sinclair, Director of the First Congregational Church Weekday Preschool and Kindergarten in Winter Park, Florida, notes that the latest discoveries on how the brain learns support what Jean Piaget discovered through observation decades ago—that children learn best through play-based experiences. "One of our favorite mottos comes from a great leader in the field of early childhood education, Bev Bos: 'If it hasn't been in the hand, it can't be in the brain,'" Ms. Sinclair says.

Pretend play is especially valuable in guiding young children to learn social conventions and to explore their emotions and the emotional responses of others. Make-believe play presents many opportunities for children to explore naturally how people may respond differently to the same situations, what consequences their actions may have on other people's emotions, and what behaviors signal different emotions. In pretend play, children may develop empathy by considering how other people feel, what makes us different from each other, and what we all have in common. These complexities work their way into children's everyday interactions with each other in play and cooperative learning. As Hirsh-Pasek and colleagues note,

> Play helps children learn to subordinate desires to social rules, cooperate with others willingly, and engage in socially appropriate behavior—all skills vital to the demands of school. Make-believe play has been found to be crucial for building children's social competence, including their ability to self-regulate and cope emotionally. (2009, p. 38)

ADOPTING "RITUALS OF OPTIMISM"

Author Marcus Conyers shares a fond memory of an evening ritual that helped make him the optimist he is today: Every night as he was getting ready for bed, his mother would ask, "What were the best things that happened today?" Marcus's young brain would then focus on his day, working to recall the best things and to focus his thoughts on them. Then his mother would ask, "What good things do you think will happen tomorrow?" And he would peer into the potential good that might happen the next day. That little routine turned out to be a regular workout to build his lifelong capacity for optimism.

We have shared that story with tens of thousands of teachers through the years, and many educators have told us how much it meant to them. Some of them have adapted their own "optimism rituals" for themselves and their children, and some have incorporated these kinds of questions in their classrooms to help their students become more optimistic about their lives and their likelihood of doing well in school.

Along the same lines, in their work teaching students to develop and maintain an optimistic outlook, Seligman and colleagues (2007) led students through a variety of exercises to emphasize and explore the positive aspects of their lives: recalling pleasant sensory experiences, listing their strengths, and helping others. Bono and Froh (2009) have explored how guiding students to identify and share what they are grateful for in their lives elicits positive feelings and relationships. Learning to say "thank you" makes others feel good—and reinforces children's own positive emotions and feelings of community.

Engaging With Educators

Christena Nelson illustrates the importance of an optimistic outlook for her kindergartners at Copper Canyon Elementary School in West Jordan, Utah, with a puppet show featuring the characters Tess the Treasure Hunter (who represents the power of positive thinking) and Gus the Grumpy Garbage Collector. The puppets get the children's attention and make the lesson about the benefits of looking on the bright side much more memorable.

"I ask them, 'Which one are you? Are you Tess the Treasure Hunter? Or are you Gus the Grumpy Garbage Collector?' They all say, 'We're Tess! We're Tess!'" And when someone starts to get negative, Ms. Nelson tells the class generally, taking care not to single out any one student, "Uh-oh! Looking like we've got Gus the Grumpy Garbage Collector in class today."

"It's really helpful to remind students of the power of thinking positively," she says.

Emphasizing the positive characteristics of oneself and others, regularly expressing gratitude, and complimenting others are also among exercises Davidson (2012) recommends for people who want to reshape their emotional outlook to become more optimistic. These rituals and exercises are beneficial for both children and adults, and introducing them at a young age may help instill attitudes and outlooks that persist throughout one's life. As one example, researchers have found that community service and volunteering to help others also benefits the volunteers, especially older adults, who tend to have better physical and mental health and greater life satisfaction than their peers who do not volunteer. The Corporation for National and Community Service notes that the health benefits of volunteering have a "threshold," variously defined by different researchers as requiring service with two or more organizations or putting in between 1 and 2 hours of volunteer work per week.

In her book *Positivity*, Barbara Frederickson (2009) makes the case that maintaining at least a 3-to-1 ratio of positive-to-negative emotions helps people become more creative and more resilient in difficult times. Instead of letting outside forces dictate how you feel and which emotions guide your actions, Frederickson suggests that "you can tip the scales to unleash your life's potential to flourish" (p. 11). She goes on to explain:

> Whatever your current circumstances, you've got what it takes to reshape your life and the world around you for the better. You have, already within you, the active ingredient that's needed to craft a happy life that's full of growth and creativity and to be remarkably resilient in hard times. (p. 15)

Frederickson recommends the conscious cultivation of 10 positive emotions and energies: joy, gratitude, serenity, interest, hope, pride, amusement, inspiration, awe, and love. Achor (2010) concurs: "When we are happy—when our mindset and mood are positive—we are smarter, more motivated, and thus more successful. Happiness is the center, and success revolves around it" (p. 37). Because these emotions are contagious, in the best sense of that word, early childhood educators and parents should seek out opportunities to help young children experience these emotions as well!

TO TEACH OPTIMISM, EMBRACE IT IN YOURSELF

To underscore an essential point, teachers and parents need to be optimists to teach young children to adopt an optimistic outlook in their approach to learning and life. What you think about young children's abilities to learn and thrive matters. Hattie (2009) writes that creating a positive learning environment

> requires teachers to enter the classroom with certain conceptions about progress, relationships, and students. It requires them to believe that their role is that of a change agent—that all students *can* learn and progress, that achievement for all is changeable and not fixed, and that demonstrating to all students that they care about their learning is both powerful and effective. (p. 128)

He makes a similar case for educating parents

> in the language of schooling, so that the home and school can share in the expectations, and the child does not have to live in two worlds. . . .

It is not so much the structure of the family but rather the beliefs and expectations of the adults in the home that contributes most to achievement. (pp. 70–71)

HOW TO NURTURE YOUR OWN INNER "BRIGHTSIDE"

Achor (2010) offers several everyday strategies that early childhood educators and parents may find effective in developing and maintaining a more positive outlook:

- *Learning to meditate.* Even 5 minutes a day of focused meditation can help you achieve a state of calm contentment, relief from stress, heightened awareness, and empathy. Meditation is a form of "downtime" that may help clear the mind and refuel your creative energy for discovering novel solutions to formidable challenges.
- *Looking forward to something you enjoy.* Anticipation of future rewards, such as a planned vacation or other event, can boost endorphin levels, the brain chemicals associated with feelings of pleasure, as much as the actual experience.
- *Committing acts of kindness.* Deliberate and conscious altruism involving family, friends, or strangers alike produces psychological benefits. Achor notes that even small gestures, such as paying the toll of the driver behind you, can decrease stress and make you feel good about yourself.
- *Infusing positive feelings into your surroundings.* Arrange your office to take advantage of a pleasant view. Make sure you get outside regularly for some fresh air. Take a walk on a sunny day. Reduce your exposure to negative TV viewing and other media.
- *Exercising.* Brisk workouts support peak Body-Brain System functioning and produce an endorphin boost that enhances positive feelings.
- *Engaging in a signature strength.* You might find great pleasure in baking your special muffins that always get rave reviews from family and friends or in framing photographs you took while traveling. When author Donna Wilson travels to a university town, she tries to arrange her schedule so she can spend some time immersed in research and reading at the education library. That is her way of indulging in her love of learning about learning and sharing her discoveries with other educators.

Cultivating Optimism

Developing and maintaining an optimistic outlook will help young children be more open to undertake learning challenges and persist through obstacles and setbacks to achieve mastery. Through these strategies, you can guide children to embrace positivity in their learning endeavors and relationships with others:

- *Seek out and share examples of positivity in action.* The story of Brightside the Optimistic Puppy, the story of the Little Engine That Could, and many other children's stories illustrate the power of optimism in action.
- *Model optimism through persistent effort.* Applaud the outlook when children exhibit positivity in their playtime and learning activities and when interacting with their peers.
- *Provide children with opportunities to achieve mastery.* Plan learning activities in manageable steps, and celebrate small successes on the way to achieving a big goal. Provide children with choices and invite them to participate in planning group activities, which enhances their feelings of control.
- *Emphasize positive emotions and experiences.* In outdoor activities and nature walks, encourage children to breathe in the fresh air, to smell the flowers, to run and play and enjoy their surroundings. At snack time, emphasize the pleasure of munching on healthy snacks. Laugh together. Underscore the importance of saying "please" and "thank you." Invite children to think and talk about their favorite people, places, and things to do.
- *Examine your own emotional outlook.* Reflect on your attitudes about children's learning potential and your expectations about their behaviors and learning progress. As we explored in this chapter, educational research shows that parents' and teachers' expectations have a powerful influence on how well children learn.

FIVE

Playing with Language

The Power of Conversation and Reading Aloud

Perhaps you know a 4-year-old like this one: He chatters away, stringing complex sentences together with ease and using a broad descriptive vocabulary that includes words like "fascinating," "apparently," and "humongous." He can readily tell you which dinosaurs were carnivores and which were herbivores, and he'll opine enthusiastically about why the Triceratops is his absolute favorite. Some might classify this child as gifted, and certainly his verbal dexterity indicates an agile and curious mind. But his verbal skills are not primarily the product of innate intellect but of a language-rich environment in which adults and older children have spoken with him, sung to him, and read to him from the very first days of his life. This early exposure to language will likely translate to this child becoming an avid reader as well.

Words conveyed in generous portions to babies and toddlers are vital to just how well they acquire language skills. Babies enter the world with vast potential for communicating, but it is up to the adults in their lives to initiate the conversation. Psychologists Lev Vygotsky and Jerome Bruner both wrote of the impact of the child's social group on language and cognitive development—that language growth flows from tutor–learner interactions (Bruner, 1966) and that the conversations young children have with and hear from their families and others close to them becomes their inner language that supports their thought processes (Vygotsky, 1986). By listening to the people who interact with them, young children build their vocabularies, gain knowledge of phonemes, and learn the basics of grammatical structure.

THE BEGINNINGS OF LANGUAGE

The acquisition of language is an example of the body and brain working together, as described in Chapter 3. Oral language requires the use of the lungs, larynx, vocal cords, tongue, lips, and jaw to produce sound and articulate speech. However, speech originates in the brain—specifically in two key areas of the frontal lobe. **Broca's area** is associated with the production of speech and other linguistic functions, while **Wernicke's area** has been identified as integral to language comprehension. Aamodt and Wang (2011) explain that maturation of the brain regions that control movement is required before speech production is possible. In addition, fine motor control is necessary to create sounds of language that can be understood.

Neuroplasticity facilitates the ability of infants and toddlers to acquire language. Research indicates that the brain actually "rewires" itself to allow for language development (Eliot, 1999). Babies start with the potential to learn any language, but they soon become more and more sensitive to the language they hear spoken every day. Within just a few months, their receptivity to other languages fades as their preference for their native language grows.

Language development starts in infancy, when children are newly exposed to language, and progresses to the complex processing that is evident in 3-year-olds, the age at which children are typically able to engage in sophisticated conversation (Kuhl & Rivera-Gaxiola, 2008). Even before babies develop the ability to talk, they are listening to their parents, siblings, and other people in their lives. They are especially receptive to the distinctive high-pitched, singsongy style of talking known as motherese, described in Chapter 1. They attempt to mimic the speech they hear through cooing, babbling, and some vocalization of vowels and consonants.

Most infants start saying their first words around their first birthday, with nouns being learned the earliest (Goodman, Dale, & Li, 2008). As they move toward their second birthday, they start combining words to convey simple thoughts ("More juice," "Doggie run," etc.) and progress toward simple sentences. There is considerable variance in how many words a toddler will speak in the first 2 to 3 years of life. On average, however, an 18-month-old can say 50 to 100 words. In the ensuing months, the rate of vocabulary acquisition in most young children sky-rockets. Between the ages of 2 and 3, their vocabulary will grow to up-ward of 500 words (Fenson, Marchman, Thal, Dale, Reznick, & Bates, 2007). They also develop more complex language abilities, including the use of spatial concepts, pronouns, descriptions, plurals, and past-tense verbs. In fact, children at a young age (under 6 or 7) are more capable of absorbing language, especially the rules and logic of grammar, than older children (Eliot, 1999).

As they gain language skills, children in these early years also become accustomed to the prosody of everyday speech. As previously described in Chapter 3, "prosody" refers to the rhythm and intonation of spoken language, which is often just as important to conveying meaning as the words themselves. As is the case with other aspects of speech develop-ment, children develop prosody from listening to others speak.

From ages 3 to 5, language development proceeds concurrently with the beginnings of literacy development. Literacy skills are built from many of the same activities as other forms of language development, such as listening to and speaking words in conversations with parents, teachers, and other children. Equally important for children this age is being read to by adults and being able to explore books on their own. Researchers have determined that frequent story reading by parents, cou-pled with the child's engagement in that experience at the age of 24 months, plays a key role in future literacy and language development (Crain-Thoreson & Dale, 1992). In this chapter, we will explore just how important adult input has been proven to be as children explore their emerging language, reading, and writing abilities.

30 MILLION WORDS

The input of spoken language is essential to developing the neural con-nections that are vital for language acquisition and cognitive thinking. A continuous flow of words from adults' lips to babies' and toddlers' ears has been found to be an important indicator of just how well children will acquire language, how varied their vocabulary will be, and how pre-pared they will be for learning.

Hart and Risley (2003) conducted what is regarded as the seminal study on this subject, following 42 families with young children and tabulating the number of words spoken in the home during one-hour visits on a monthly basis. They did this for 2½ years, starting when the children were between the ages of 7 and 9 months and concluding about the time of their third birthdays. The study encompassed families from all socioeconomic groups, and researchers found significant correlations between the number of words that children heard spoken at home and the earning power of parents. Children in the highest socioeconomic group heard on average 2,153 words per hour spoken, compared to an average 1,251 words per hour heard by children in families of middle to lower socioeconomic status (SES) and an average 616 words per hour heard by children whose family relied on welfare.

Extrapolating this gap in language exposure over the first 4 years of life, a child in a high-SES family would have accumulated exposure to almost 45 million words, compared to 26 million words for a child in a middle to lower SES family and just 13 million words for a child in a poor family. That's a gap of *more than 30 million words*.

All of this word counting led to several related findings, chief among them that the children with the least amount of language exposure had smaller vocabularies than the children raised in language-rich environments. In addition, the gaps continued to widen as the children grew older. Moreover, the researchers found that vocabulary use of children in the study at age 3 was highly predictive of their language skills at the ages of 9 and 10. Thus, the need for attention to development is critical at an early age.

Another study, this one targeted at lower-income families, reached similar conclusions about the importance of language exposure and conversations in the development of young children—not only at home but also in preschool classrooms (Dickinson & Tabors, 2002). Known as the Home–School Study of Language and Literacy Development, this in-depth examination followed 74 low-income children in their preschool years with the goal of identifying how homes and preschool programs could help build a strong foundation in language and literacy.

Through audiotaped conversations with mothers and teachers, the study identified three key criteria that relate to later literacy success: (1) exposure to a large and varied vocabulary; (2) opportunities to participate in conversations that use extended discourse; and (3) creation of environments, both at home and in the classroom, that are cognitively and linguistically stimulating. A large part of creating a stimulating environment is to have many books present and to make reading aloud part of the norm. As Dickinson and Tabors (2002) explain:

> Children are most likely to experience conversations that include comprehensible and interesting extended discourse and are rich with vocabulary when their parents are able to obtain and read good books and when their teachers provide classrooms with a curriculum that is varied and stimulating. (p. 12–13)

The Home–School Study of Language and Literacy Development supports essentially the same conclusion as Hart and Risley's work (2003); namely, children need to hear language early and often. **Nonimmediate talk**, or conversing with children in ways that extend reading experiences, appears to be especially useful in helping them develop their literacy skills. DeTemple (2001) describes nonimmediate talk as conversations using text and illustrations in picture books "as a springboard for recollections of personal experiences, comments, or questions about general knowledge or for drawing inferences and making predictions" (p. 37). This type of talk tends to use more complex language, to make connections well beyond the stories read, to tie what is read to children's experiences, and to explore more abstract concepts. Children of parents participating in the Home–School Study who used more nonimmediate talk after reading scored higher than their peers in measures of language and early literacy when they entered school. These findings add to the evidence that exposure to a large quantity and variety of words in the early stages of life builds vocabulary, sets children on a path to better verbal skills, and prepares them for the next exciting step in their developmental journey—learning to read.

In addition to highlighting the importance of talk related to reading experiences, the Home–School Study also underscores the utility of everyday conversations among children and parents, children and teachers in early childhood programs, and children talking to each other:

> The conversations that children have during the classroom day when they are 3 and 4 years old are related to a broad range of skills using oral language and print at the end of kindergarten. . . . We found more evidence of effects of teachers' behaviors during group times and more evidence of children's impact on each other during free play. (Dickinson, 2001b, p. 251)

FACILITATING READING READINESS

Children who love to read are likely to become adults who love to read. Reading aloud to young children is widely recognized as an important way of building a lifelong love of books. Parents, caregivers, and teachers who read aloud to children form a connection and pave a path toward literacy. Reading is the conduit to magical places, both real and imagined, that are conveyed through the near-endless combinations of 26 letters that young prereaders look forward to mastering. Through the power of storytelling, children explore the world around them and learn about important concepts found frequently in children's books and literature, such as honesty, friendship, loyalty, and courage.

Researchers have found that children's success in reading is strongly affected by the skills they acquire during their formative years. For instance, early oral language skills directly relate to reading outcomes in preschool and early elementary school. Specifically, early oral language abilities have been found to be important not only for building preliteracy skills such as phonological awareness and letter-word skills but also in contributing to reading comprehension (NICHD Early Child Care Research Network, 2005).

The relationship between oral language skills and reading is largely reciprocal. Children with strong oral skills are better prepared to read books, but a strong home literacy environment is required to develop strong oral skills. Storch and Whitehurst (2001) observe that children whose home environments lack shared reading activities and print materials are likely to have poor oral language skills. This literacy deficit can have a snowball effect, given that there is a strong relationship between preschool oral language and **code-related skills** (the ability to decode and encode text). Code-related skills are important for reading achievement, and thus the lack of those skills puts children at risk for later reading difficulties (Storch & Whitehurst, 2002).

Learning to read requires the integration of many brain functions. As would be expected, the visual cortex is vital in the emergent reader's ability to perceive written letters and words and process the meaning of text. Perhaps not quite so obviously, auditory processing plays a role as well. Language development requires the rapid processing of auditory stimuli. Interestingly, the temporal lobe (in particular, Wernicke's area) is highly active during reading and processes information as if one were listening to spoken words (Wilson & Conyers, 2009).

Building Blocks for Literacy

The process of learning to read builds on language skills that a child already possesses. Teachers and parents can support these efforts by using language that is appropriate to the language level of the child. This process is called **scaffolding** and involves using language that is at the same time understandable and challenging to the child. Scaffolding can involve shortening complex sentences or using simpler vocabulary. Such strategies help wire the brain for language skills and help children learn to read more effectively (Wilson & Conyers, 2009). At the same time, though, introducing children to more complex words and syntax supports continual language development.

Young children often clamor to read their favorite books again and again, which appears to enhance language skills. As DeTemple (2001) notes:

> Repeated readings and discussions of the same page in a book are rich settings for language acquisition. It may be that a certain level of talk occurs with unfamiliar books and that repeated, shared readings are necessary for more complex, elaborate language . . . to emerge. (p. 42)

Before children can learn to read on their own, they must master some basic prereading skills. It's important, for example, that they have **phonemic awareness**—the ability to hear and identify the smallest structural units of sound in a language. In English, examples are the /b/ in *ball*, the /ch/ in *chair*, and the /oo/ in *boot*. Phonemic awareness is a key skill that is required in reading and writing. Early childhood educators can strengthen phonemic awareness by having children identify words that start with a particular sound (such as /b/ for *ball*, *boy*, and *baby*) or contain a certain vowel sound (such as /oo/ for *book*, *look*, and *moon*). A key prereading skill is to match sounds to letters and letters to words. In addition, broader-based phonological processing skills, which involve the ability to identify and apply the sounds of language—have been found to be strongly related to children's emergent literacy (Wilson & Conyers, 2009).

Research supports the premise that story reading with parents and early reading instruction contribute to the development of literacy (Crain-Thoreson & Dale, 1992). In that same study, researchers cited the positive impact of instruction in letter names and sounds during the preschool years, as it strongly predicts children's knowledge of print conventions, recognition of invented spelling, and phonological awareness before they enter kindergarten.

Books, Books, and More Books

Beyond familiarizing them with letters and print conventions, regularly reading to preschoolers "helps prepare children for school by building their vocabulary, introducing them to strategies for understanding books, and teaching them to participate in group activities that involve talking and listening" (Dickinson, 2001a, p. 200). To accomplish those worthy aims, researchers with the Home–School Study recommend that early childhood programs do the following:

- Include one or two sessions each day of reading books aloud for at least 10 minutes for half-day programs and three reading sessions per day in full-day schedules.
- Divide larger groups into small reading groups of 8 to 10 children for some reading times so children can be encouraged to ask questions and talk with their teachers and other children about the stories.
- Where possible, read with children individually, and schedule times for children to look at books on their own and with friends.
- Read and reread favorite books and books that reflect a theme you may be exploring with other play and learning activities.
- Read with drama, varied intonation, and humor. Ask questions to gauge children's understanding of the story, and invite them to ask their own questions and share stories that relate to the book topic.

Familiarity With the Act of Book Reading

The process of reading to children helps familiarize them with various print conventions associated with books and reading—that is, that books have a title page and an author and that reading proceeds from the first to the final page, from the top to the bottom of the page, and from left to right on each line. Even though they cannot read themselves, young children enjoy handling a book, looking at the pictures, and turning the pages.

Many children's books have special features that enhance the reading experience in entertaining ways. So-called board books are designed especially for babies and young children with thick, sturdy pages, vivid illustrations, and large print. Some books also feature tactile surfaces that are designed to encourage the child to interact with the pages—such as the scratchy feel of a frog's tongue, the soft fur of a kitten or bunny, and the rough, bumpy skin of a frog or lizard. Pop-up books provide an added dimension to reading that is surprising and fun for young readers. Still other books come accompanied by a stuffed animal or doll version of the main character. Beloved literary characters like Curious George or Madeline are more than mere characters in a book. They become cherished playthings whose stories young children commit to their emerging memories but nonetheless beg to read again and again.

The role of early childhood educators, parents, and caregivers in teaching emergent young readers is as much cheerleader as instructor. Young children are susceptible to feedback, whether positive or negative. In fact, failing readers may be stymied even further by their own poor perception of their abilities. As Cambourne (2001a) observed:

> The evidence from the literature on self-esteem and expectations strongly indicates that the majority of failed readers have low expectations of themselves as readers and writers. . . . If a response continually communicates negative messages about the novice as learner, or about learning performance, then the novice is likely to cease engaging with future demonstrations of what he or she is attempting to learn. (pp. 785–786)

FUN WITH LANGUAGE

In Chapter 3, we explained that children achieve much of their early learning through play and therefore are more likely to give their full attention to an activity that has an element of fun. When teaching language and literacy skills, teachers and parents can make use of such useful devices as rhyme and alliteration to add fun to the learning experience.

Rhymes are certainly a time-tested way of teaching language, as reliable and beloved as Mother Goose herself. Nursery rhymes such as Humpty Dumpty and Jack and Jill are short and memorable, lending themselves to group recitation. Children also love the works of the incomparable Dr. Seuss, who used witty rhymes to teach and entertain in dozens of best-selling books such as *The Cat in the Hat*, *Horton Hears a Who!*, and *How the Grinch Stole Christmas*.

Teachers, parents, and caregivers can help children ages 3 through 5 grasp the concept of rhyming by asking them to come up with groups of rhyming words. Start with the /at/ sound, for example. Ask children to shout out words that end in that sound: *bat*, *hat*, *cat*, and *mat*. Or share drawings of animals and objects that represent rhyming words and ask children to connect the pictures that represent words that sound alike.

Alliteration is another fun way to play with language while also teaching children phonemes. Most 3- and 4-year-olds know the first letter of their first name, so a good way to teach alliteration would be to encourage them to come up with an alliterative adjective that goes with their name. For instance, "My name is Sophia, and I'm sassy." Or, "My name is Eric, and I'm excellent." Given that children's vocabulary is limited at this age, adults should be ready to step in with suggestions. Be sure to note the children's answers, and for the rest of the day, call them by their adjectives: "Okay, Excellent Eric, it's time to take your seat now."

There are plenty of fun tongue twisters that use alliteration, such as the classic "Peter Piper picked a peck of pickled peppers" and "How much wood would a woodchuck chuck if a woodchuck could chuck wood?" These might be pretty tough for a 3-year-old, but a 4-year-old should be able to master them quite nicely with a little practice. Children also can have a great deal of fun singing songs that teach them more about words and language. Of course, there is the classic "ABC Song." Other simultaneously fun and educational songs include "Apples and Bananas," which plays with language to teach children their vowel sounds, and "Old MacDonald Had a Farm," which helps children match up animals with the sounds they make.

While teaching children age-appropriate words is important, you can also occasionally throw in a really big word to see if they can grasp it. Children who have seen *Mary Poppins* may have already experienced the fun of saying or singing "Supercalifragilisticexpialidocious!" Many young children love to wrap their tongue around nonsense words like that, though you can also introduce them to actual words like "chrysanthemum" or "photosynthesis" that will be fun for them to say while also expanding their vocabulary. We recommend introducing words that convey use of cognitive skills, such as attention (Chapter 3), optimism (Chapter 4), and comparison (Chapter 6), as children learn about and practice these learning strategies.

Engaging With Educators

Learning to read in Regina Cabadaidis's pre-K and kindergarten class is a multisensory experience, starting with the visual but also encompassing the auditory and the tactile. "Everything is labeled in my classroom," reports Ms. Cabadaidis, who teaches children ages 3 to 6 at S. D. Spady Elementary School, a Montessori magnet school in Delray Beach, Florida. "For instance, we label the directions north, south, east, and west. We label the different areas—the practical life area is labeled, the science area is labeled. There are letters and words everywhere."

High-frequency sight words are posted in the classroom. "Originally, I put the words up too high," Ms. Cabadaidis reports, "and the children came to me and said, 'We can't see the words.'"

She conferred with her students, and together they came up with the idea of putting the words on the vertical front of her desk. "I took strips of Velcro and put the words down the front of my desk in alphabetical order, so now when they need them, they can pull them off and physically take them. This turned out to be a pretty neat idea."

Ms. Cabadaidis is a big advocate of using the Montessori sandpaper letters, which allow children to both see and feel the letters of the alphabet. "If it's the letter A, they see the letter, they trace the letter, they feel the letter," she explains. "It's a very tactile experience—very hand to mind. We tell the children that the letter is A, and the sound it makes is /a/, and then they repeat after us. We have all the letters, A through Z, grouped in a specific way. We have object pictures that correspond to all the letters, so they experience the letters and the sounds they make in a variety of different ways."

LEARNING HOW TO LEARN

Emphasizing Listening Skills

Listening is one skill that young children will need to develop in order to make the most of learning opportunities. As noted in Chapter 3, it's hard for children to learn when they are not paying attention. Unfortunately, many children enter kindergarten without an understanding of the need to focus their attention and listen because they have never been taught these skills. In fact, many people may believe that children are naturally equipped with the skills and strategies they need to optimize learning, but this is not true. However, through explicit instruction and **modeling** (demonstrating appropriate behavior and social skills), the vast majority of children can be taught how to learn by applying skills such as those presented in this text (Wilson & Conyers, 2011b). To emphasize the importance of listening, for example, early childhood educators, parents, and caregivers may point out to preschoolers that when they talk to each other, people also take turns listening. They can model and demonstrate that communicating is about both talking *and* listening.

Many times, children learn to listen because the adults in their life take the time to listen to them. When talking to a child one on one, sit in a chair or crouch down to her level so that you can make eye contact. Looking the child in the eye is an excellent way to show interest and make her feel that what she has to say is important enough for your full attention. You may need to underscore that having a conversation involves taking turns. You will listen to her when she is talking, but you expect her to listen to you when it is your turn to talk.

When talking to a group of children during a lesson or classroom setting, let them know that you expect them to listen when you speak but that you will give them an opportunity to ask questions or offer their opinions when you are through. It's important that children respect each other's opportunity to speak by not interrupting. To avoid children speaking over each other, you may introduce the practice of raising hands before speaking—which will likely come in handy when they enter school! Another way to help children listen is to have them sit in a circle and roll a ball to one other or pass around a stuffed animal. Whoever has possession gets the opportunity to speak uninterrupted until rolling the ball or passing the toy to another child in the circle.

Young children have short periods of high-level attention. A key to holding their attention and ensuring that they are listening is to make sure you are speaking at a level they understand. When reading aloud to children, make sure the books are age-appropriate to hold their interest. For preschoolers, large-format books with few words and lots of pictures are the most appropriate. Make it an interactive experience by asking questions at appropriate intervals in the story.

Finally, make sure you reward children when they listen well by acknowledging how they are using this cognitive asset. A simple announcement—"Thank you for being such good listeners!"—underscores the importance of this learning skill. The story of Calm Cool, the Listening Rabbit, exemplifies this lesson well (see Textbox 5.1).

Textbox 5.1. Learn With Us

The Story of Calm Cool, the Listening Rabbit

Message: Learning to listen carefully can offer big rewards!
Key words to introduce: listening

Calm Cool is the best listener in Happy Warren School. But this was not always so.

Do you know why Calm Cool became such a good listener?

Because he *loves* carrots.

Now all rabbits like carrots, but Calm Cool *loves* them. He loves carrots because they are bright orange. He loves carrots because they are crunchy. He loves carrots because they are so *delicious*.

What Calm Cool does not love is how hard it is to find the best carrots in the school garden.

One day, Calm Cool was sitting with his friend Naughty Paws as their teacher, Ms. Hare, was teaching everyone about taking care of the garden. All the rabbits were listening carefully except for Calm Cool and Naughty Paws. Instead of listening, they were giggling and playing silly rabbit games. So they did not hear Ms. Hare when she whispered a secret: "The best carrots are in the middle of the garden, right behind the big oak tree."

When the school bell rang for play and snack time, all the other rabbits ran to the middle of the garden. Calm Cool and Naughty Paws did not run to the garden. They ran to the fence. They played hopscotch. They played shadow games with their big bunny ears.

When they finally went to the garden to get a snack, all the best carrots were gone.

"Why didn't anyone tell us there were such yummy carrots in the garden?" Calm Cool wailed as he watched his friends munching on delicious, crunchy, orange carrots.

"Ms. Hare did tell us, silly," said Digger Dan before taking another big bite of his carrot. "You just weren't listening."

The next day, Calm Cool decided he would be the best listening rabbit he could be. He kept his eyes on Ms. Hare, not on Naughty Paws. He pointed his long bunny ears right at his teacher, even though all the rabbits around him were busy boasting about the yummy carrots they found yesterday. So when Ms. Hare leaned forward to share another secret, Calm Cool was the only one listening. Ms. Hare whispered, "Today the best carrots in the garden are behind the rose bush."

When the bell rang, Calm Cool was the first one through the door. He ran to the rose bush in the garden and found the brightest, crunchiest, most delicious carrot he had ever seen. Calm Cool thought, "Life is really good when you learn to be calm and cool so you can listen carefully!"

And that is how Calm Cool became the best listener in Happy Warren School.

Activity: Play a listening game: Go outside for a "listening minute"; direct children to sit silently for a whole minute and listen and then share what they have heard. Choose a "word of the day" and give children a sticker every time they hear someone use that word. Or playing a rhyming game in which children listen for the rhyming words in silly sentences ("The mouse built a house. The dog licked the fog. The duck said, 'Cluck!'").

These stories are adapted with permission from the *Thinking for Reading Curriculum*, by Donna Wilson and Marcus Conyers (BrainSMART, 2005).

LETTERS AND WORDS EVERYWHERE

A key to the developing literacy of young children is to ensure that they are surrounded by the alphabet and words in diverse aspects of their life. Magnetic letters, which adhere to refrigerators or dry-erase boards, are a fun diversion for toddlers and preschoolers. If they are just learning to spell their names, they will love to pick out the letters and arrange them on the magnetic surface. In groups, children can have fun searching through the letters together. Two children—let's call them Jocelyn and Jacob—may even notice that their names begin with the same letter.

This is just one aspect of a print-rich environment that early childhood educators and parents should be encouraging both in a classroom environment and at home. Classrooms are particularly great places to post the letters of the alphabet, both upper- and lowercase, with corresponding pictures. These connections can be reinforced with regular group recitations ("*A* is for apple, *B* is for banana, *C* is for cat," etc.). There are opportunities all around the room to place different forms of print, such as labeling various items by their name—table, chair, toy box—and labeling containers with their contents—blocks, crayons, play tools, and so on. Children's cubbies should also have placards with their names, and teachers can display wall stories, labeled murals, and word displays. Children in classrooms such as these spontaneously use almost twice as much print in their play as those not exposed to a print-rich environment; environments filled with letters and words are effective in encouraging reading as well as the earliest stages of writing (Wilson & Conyers, 2009).

All of these methods are consistent with the immersion theory of learning, which provides multiple opportunities for students to experience visual saturation of print and text and oral saturation of the sounds of written language. Cambourne (2001b) recommends several immersion strategies, including making functional use of wall print through what he calls "print walks" and also supporting a variety of reading experiences, such as the teacher reading aloud, shared reading, taped books, and choral reading of such text as poems, rhymes, and songs from wall print.

Print-rich environments in child-care centers make an important contribution to a child's interest in learning to read (Strickland et al., 2004). Play areas and centers designed and equipped for pretend play can emphasize how reading and writing are part of daily life. For instance, if the room features a play kitchen or restaurant, props such as memo pads, recipes, and cookbooks can help children incorporate print into their playtime interactions.

In Table 5.1, we apply the AEIOU learning cycle to the early stages of literacy. For children just learning to read and write, the model is a helpful tool for furthering their recognition and use of spoken and written language.

Table 5.1. AEIOU in Action: Emerging Literacy

A	Awareness	Four-year-old Josh loves to see the letter *J* in print. "Look," he says as he points to the new classroom calendar. "That word starts with a *J*." "Yes," the teacher confirms. "That word is *January*. It's the first month of the new year, and it starts with a *J*, same as your name. Can you hear how both words start with a /j/ sound?" "Uh-huh!" Josh says excitedly. "*J* for Josh, and *J* for January."
E	Exploration	"Can you think of other words that start with the /j/ sound?" the teacher asks. "Jump!" says Josh as he jumps in the air. "That's right," the teacher says. "Jupiter," he says as he runs to the poster of the planets hanging on the wall. "Right again," the teacher agrees.
I	Inquiry	"Giraffe!" says Josh as he points to the cover of a book depicting zoo animals. "Actually," the teacher says, "*giraffe* starts with the letter *G*. *G* is one of those special letters that makes more than one sound. Sometimes, it sounds like /j/ as in *giraffe*, and sometimes it sounds like /g/ as in *girl*." "So, there are letters that make the same sound, even though they're different?" Josh asks. "That's correct," the teacher affirms.
O	Order	"I think we have a book will help us come up with more ideas," the teacher says. She finds an alphabet picture book, and together they turn to the page for the letter *J*. "Wow," says Josh as he points to the pictures. "Jet, juice, jam, jellyfish . . ."
U	Understanding/ Use	Josh squints at the final picture. "Pumpkin?" The teacher shares a reminder, "Remember, all the words start with the /j/ sound." "Oh, yeah," Josh says with a laugh. "It's a jack-o-lantern."

FUTURE READERS AND WRITERS

Although some children become readers and writers before entering kindergarten, most are more accurately described as "pre-readers" or "emergent readers" (Strickland & Shanahan, 2004).

Learning to read, taken in conjunction with learning to write, is a process known commonly as **emerging literacy**. As in language development, the key to emerging literacy is regular exposure to meaningful activities, both written and spoken. Reading aloud to children is just one component that sets the stage for eventual literacy. It's also important to let children see and interact with written words in everyday situations and to provide them with the opportunity to practice the act of reading and writing (Wilson & Conyers, 2009).

Early reading is a powerful indicator of future reading. Children who have early success in reading are likely to spend a considerable time doing it, whereas those who read poorly are likely to get frustrated and do as little of it as possible. A gap, which only widens as time goes on, develops between the successful readers and the unsuccessful readers. This creates a phenomenon known as the "Matthew effect," taken from the biblical passage that describes how the rich get richer and the poor get poorer (Stanovich, 1986). Successful readers get an intrinsic reward from their reading. The more they enjoy reading, the more they practice it, and the more they practice it, the better they get at it. Poor readers, who already are struggling because of poor decoding skills, fall further behind due to lack of practice. Not only do their reading skills suffer, but their lack of exposure to books also deters their vocabulary growth and their exposure to general knowledge gained through books.

A 10-year longitudinal study confirmed that those who get off to a fast start in reading are more likely to read more over the years (Cunningham & Stanovich, 1998). The study found that a higher volume of reading has positive effects even on children with modest cognitive abilities by building their vocabulary and general knowledge. The researchers determined that those who read a lot enhance their verbal intelligence—"that is, reading will make them smarter" (p. 14).

Just as children are emerging in reading, they also begin their first attempts at writing. They typically start off with drawings and scribbles, which are precursors to written language. Children often use the letters of their name as an early basis for writing other words. In their early writing attempts, children may use a beginning letter to represent the whole word. This progresses to the addition of ending letters and then vowels within the words. Children's first successful attempts at spelling will be with high-frequency words (e.g., *the*, *and*, *it*, etc.) and later with words that they sound out phonetically. This is a painstaking process; thus, it's important that children find writing meaningful and enjoyable. Observing other people writing and participating in literacy activities make writing more purposeful and gratifying (Wilson & Conyers, 2009).

☆*PRACTICAL TIPS FOR EARLY CHILDHOOD EDUCATORS*☆

Cultivating Language Acquisition and Emerging Literacy

Discovering the world of language and the printed word is exciting for young children. To understand words written on a page—and to realize that they can make themselves understood through speaking and writing—is a truly profound development for children in their preschool years. Early childhood educators are there to witness, instruct, and guide these children toward their newfound power—the power to speak, to read, to communicate. These kinds of activities can aid in that endeavor:

Vocabulary builder. Hart and Risley (2003) cite an interesting statistic from their famous study: 86% to 98% of the words recorded in each child's vocabulary came from their parents' vocabulary. Here's what you as an educator can do to expand children's vocabularies.

- Use rare words that children are unlikely to encounter in everyday conversations. Recast their sentences or expound on their thoughts with more descriptive language and more grammatically sophisticated sentences (Roskos, Christie, & Richgels, 2003).
- Whenever you encounter an unusual word during read-aloud sessions, stop and ask the children if they know what it means. Provide positive feedback if someone in the group knows the word, but encourage creative guesses before providing the answer. Talk about the word in context of the story and explore the relevance of the word to the children's lives.
- Take a tip from those "Word of the Day" calendars. Introduce children to one new word each day. Write the word on a dry-erase board. Lead the children in a recitation of the spelling of the word and also define the word. Provide encouragement when they use the word during the course of the day or even a few days later: "Wow, I'm impressed. You remembered the word *nutritious* we learned the other day. That's great!"

Emergent reading. We can't stress enough the importance of reading aloud to children. As preschoolers, they are still in the prereading stage, and in these years, you are doing the important work of setting the stage for future enthusiasm and the skill acquisition required for reading.

- Create a cozy library nook, stocked with plenty of books for beginning readers, and make it as inviting as possible with pillows, stuffed animals, dolls, and other comfortable embellishments (Strickland et al., 2004).
- Have functional print linked to classroom activities, such as the daily schedules, helper charts, and labels on the toy shelves (Roskos et al., 2003).
- Use large-format storybooks that are easy for the children to follow. Turn the book around so that children can see the pictures that go along with the words. Stop and encourage discussions about developments in the story. Ask children to tell you what they think will happen next.
- Help teach print conventions by letting them create a "book" with folded paper. Use a handheld hole puncher on the creased area of the paper, then have the children bind their books with ribbon or yarn.

Emergent writing. Don't expect to discover any budding Hemingways or Jane Austens in your midst just yet, though a vivid imagination and storytelling abilities are precursors to writing skills. Encourage children's developing writing as much as possible. Here are a few steps for doing just that:

- Have a writing center, complete with pens, pencils, markers, crayons, paper, and so on. Encourage kids to write in whatever way they can, including scribble writing and random letters (Roskos et al., 2003).
- Encourage them to write a story about themselves through whatever means they can—drawings, scribbles, or pictures cut from magazines.
- Have a "story time," allowing kids to contribute to the story while you write the story on a big pad of paper or a dry-erase board.

SIX

Problem-Solving, Creativity, and Thinking Skills

Early Stages of Children Taking Charge of Their Learning

Psychologists studying child development have come up with some fascinating experiments to study how and when infants and toddlers begin to exhibit reasoning and problem-solving abilities. For example, Goswami (2008) summarizes experiments gauging the degree to which infants can puzzle out "impossible events" such as whether a toy bear can come from a previously empty cage or whether a small object hidden under a cloth could be a large toy dog. In another study on numerical relationships, two arrays were placed in front of infants, one with two objects and the other with three, and then researchers introduced two audio patterns, one with two drumbeats and the other three, to assess whether the infants associated the audio patterns with the arrays.

Other researchers have closely observed infants learning to use spoons as tools, first to make noise and later to feed themselves, and older children building block towers and selecting correctly from different sizes of rods to push toys through a tube. Keen (2011) concludes from these types of experiments that infants demonstrate "inklings" of the ability to plan, which is a necessary element of problem solving, and "planning ahead in order to achieve a goal is solidly present during the second year of life" (p. 2).

Early childhood educators, caregivers, and parents see this kind of cognitive development all the time—in less controlled situations, of course, but still evidence of young children's desire to interact with the world around them and achieve mastery of new motor and cognitive skills. In this chapter, we explore how we can guide young children to develop their creative and problem-solving abilities and self-regulatory behaviors to facilitate learning.

LEARNING AS A PROCESS TO CREATE SOLUTIONS

Some people think of creativity and problem solving as quite different skills, the former associated with artistic and imaginative endeavors and the latter linked to more analytical pursuits like math and science. When it comes to how young children learn and develop their cognitive abilities, however, creativity and problem solving are closely intertwined. Young children should be given every opportunity to "create solutions" to help explore their surroundings, interact with others, process new information, and hone their thinking skills and physical abilities.

Psychologists conducting studies like those mentioned at the beginning of this chapter typically look for three components in assessing whether infants and toddlers are exhibiting problem-solving behavior: (1) they want to achieve an end state or goal, (2) achieving this end state requires a sequence of mental processes, and (3) those mental processes are cognitive rather than automatic. An infant rapping a toy hammer to make noise or shaking a water-filled toy to see how the objects suspended in it move around is engaging in actions that indicate cognitive processes at work.

To understand how closely linked creativity and problem solving are, it may be useful to take a cue from what Meltzoff and colleagues (2009) refer to the "new science of learning," which applies psychology, neuroscience, and education research to how humans learn. For infants and young children, learning is both computational (for example, language is learned through the sensing of statistical patterns of phonetic units that make up one's native language) and social (infants pick up on cues from people around them about what they need to learn). In addition, "learning is supported by brain circuits linking perception and action. . . . The brain machinery needed to perceive the world and move our bodies to adapt to the movements of people and objects is complex, requiring continuous adaptation and plasticity" (p. 285).

Imitation as the Sincerest Form of Learning

As we noted in Chapter 1, infants and young children are avid imitators. Newborns just hours and days old have been shown to imitate facial movements such as sticking out their tongues when adults do the same. Of all the aspects of their surroundings, infants seem most fascinated by human faces. They observe, learn, and respond in kind to others' expressions of emotion (Davidson, 2012). They listen to and do their best to imitate spoken language and watch and imitate movements as well.

Just as they learn language and motor skills, infants and young children learn how to tackle challenges and solve problems through imitation. The experiments of Meltzoff and colleagues (2009) show how much infants and toddlers learn by imitating the actions of adults and older children. This learning is not just copying but working out goals and intentions: When 18-month-olds observed an adult trying unsuccessfully to pull apart an object, they imitated those actions—and then took to the next step of completing the task, thus demonstrating their understanding of the end goal. As the researchers note, learning by imitation offers several advantages:

> Imitation accelerates learning and multiplies learning opportunities. It is faster than individual discovery and safer than trial-and-error learning. Children can use third-person information (observation of others) to create first-person knowledge. This is an accelerator for learning: Instead of having to work out causal relations themselves, children can learn from watching experts. (p. 285)

A USEFUL TOOL IN THE COGNITIVE TOOLKIT

Of all the skills young children can learn through imitation, puzzling out how to solve problems is among the most useful. Psychologist Rachel Keen calls problem solving a critical cognitive skill that adults can and should encourage in young children (2011). The use of tools such as eating utensils and play hammers demonstrates how perception, motor skills, and cognition work together as infants begin to exhibit problem-solving abilities beginning at about 9 months. These abilities continue to develop, as evident in the sequence of plans toddlers must carry out to build taller and taller block towers. Keen calls for proper environmental conditions to allow children to hone their problem-solving abilities, noting that even "precocity needs the proper environment in early life for its expression" (p. 7).

A "proper" environment to foster the development of problem-solving skills should provide many opportunities for playful learning and exploration. Children playing on their own with objects and materials tend to come up with more creative and flexible uses for those objects than when undergoing explicit instruction from an adult, Keen notes: "Preschoolers appear to inherently enjoy problem solving. . . . Children are driven by curiosity and a need to explore" (2011, p. 18). All this playful learning has serious purpose, she concludes: "We need to equip children with planning and problem-solving skills so they are ready to meet the evermore difficult and complex problems they will encounter" later in school and in life (p. 19).

MAKING MEANING OF THE WORLD AROUND THEM

Engaging in creative and problem-solving pursuits through playful learning is a path to make meaning of new concepts and information, which is a crucial aim of the middle components of the AEIOU learning cycle—exploring, inquiring, and bringing order to newfound knowledge. This meaning making may take many forms, such as

- learning the definition and proper use of new words ("I live in Wisconsin. Do you live in Wisconsin, too?");
- developing new motor skills such as drawing ("I made a tree like the one near the swings!"); and
- improving interpersonal skills such as taking turns and sharing ("You can play with this now. I am going to build a castle.").

Children make meaning of new concepts in different ways. For example, by playing and exploring on their own at the sand table, they may discover that adding water helps sand hold a shape. While observing a friend drawing, they may realize that a circle is a good first step to draw a face. With guidance and spoken instructions from a parent, they may figure out how to swing their arms out and grab the next bar to make their way across the monkey bars. By listening to a story read by a teacher, they may come to understand how sharing benefits everyone. Thus, young children make meaning and further their learning through multiple pathways—for example, auditory, visual, and kinesthetic (Berninger & Richards, 2002; Wilson & Conyers, 2011a).

One way educators and parents can facilitate this process of meaning making is to connect new information with what children already know through past experiences. Learning is a naturally incremental process, building increasingly more sophisticated knowledge and skills on the foundation of basic abilities children have already mastered. First they must learn how to climb the ladder and then grab and hang from the first monkey bar before they take the next big step of swinging one arm to the next bar and making the transfer. In the same way, they learn first that each letter represents a sound that in combination makes a word. Then come sentences—and later whole stories and books!

Consider this example of a parent explaining the concept of a map to a 4-year-old:

Child: But our town is bigger than this little dot!

Parent: They have to make it tiny to fit everything on the map. It shows many, many towns all across the country.

Child: Huh?

Parent: OK, remember when we drove to visit Grandma D?

Child: That took a long time.

Parent: It did. Almost three hours. We drove across the state from where we live—here—to Tampa, where Grandma lives, over here.

Child: That's not very long.

Parent: No, it doesn't seem that way on this map. But remember when we drove out to see Grandpa and Grandma Jones in Arizona?

Child: That was really, really far away. We stayed in motels.

Parent: Yes, for two nights. And drove for three days. Here is Arizona on the map, so we drove all this way.

Child: So all these lines are roads for driving on?

Parent: That's right!

Child: So, how long would it take us to get here?

Parent: To Washington? Oh, that would take a really, really long time!

By connecting the concept of reading a map to trips the child had taken, her parent helps her to begin to understand the great distances that maps represent and why people might use maps to help them navigate. These are big ideas building on the child's existing knowledge about how big the world outside her door really is.

Knowledge is not something a learner passively absorbs; it must be actively created by building on connections to what she already knows. As the Center for Accelerated Learning (n.d.) puts it, "Learning is creation, not consumption." For all people, but especially for young children, the most effective way to learn is not through exposure to isolated facts, but to explore, to touch and feel, to compare—to try new things out (Piaget, 1977). That's why children should have ample opportunities to mess about with new concepts, ideas, and endeavors so they can make their own connections—and meaning (Wilson & Conyers, 2011a).

Engaging With Educators

Teachable cognitive skills take many forms, and opportunities to guide children to employ useful thinking strategies arise daily. For example, understanding spatial concepts is a cognitive skill that will serve children well in learning math and science principles—and in social situations as well. Preschool teacher Diane Hickey shares a story about a 4-year-old with left field vision loss in both eyes who was in her preschool class at Washington Elementary School in Union, New Jersey: The child had a hard time visualizing how much space he needed to navigate around other children and find a big enough spot to bring out a bin of toys at playtime.

One day, Ms. Hickey recalls, he accidentally moved between two children who were already playing and toppled their toys, evoking angry reactions. His teacher came up with the idea of providing him with a visual aid, made out of a large placemat representing the size of the space he would need for his own personal "Learning Zone." At playtime, he would take out his Learning Zone and find a spot for it on the floor before going to fetch a bin of toys.

"Within days he was able to use this mat independently and ultimately was able to invite the children that he used to annoy to play beside him," Ms. Hickey says. "When he left my class, his mother asked if she could have the mat so he could bring it to kindergarten."

ENGAGING THE SENSES IN LEARNING

Young children are naturally curious about their world, as evident in the frequency of the one-word question, "Why?" Early childhood educators and parents can answer that question by talking, explaining, and naming and counting things. But to enrich and extend these learning opportunities, adults can also encourage children to explore and engage all their senses in varied experiences. What does winter look like? Beyond the snow on the ground, it looks like bare trees and darkness falling before it's even time for dinner. What does winter feel like? Every day is cold, but some are much colder than others. Some snow is light and fluffy but not good for packing, but on other days it is perfect for building a snow fort. What does winter sound like? The rumbling of snowplows clearing the road. The rasp of the sled racing down the hill. The wind buffeting the windows during a snowstorm. What does it taste like? Encourage children to catch a flying snowflake in their mouth—but not to pick them up off the ground!

The point is that listening to adults is just one way of learning. Experiencing and experimenting with new concepts by collaborating with others, by touching, by singing, by drawing and creating—even, in some cases, by smelling and tasting—enriches learning and makes it more fun and memorable. While children are manipulating objects, engaging in pretend play, and interacting with adults and other children, they have many opportunities to reflect on new ideas, use their imaginations, and formulate answers—and new questions. When children are fully engaged in learning with all their senses, they make knowledge their own and are better able to apply what they have learned in different contexts, which is, of course, the ultimate aim of learning!

LEARNING HOW TO LEARN

Exploring Patterns, Making Connections

The human brain is a pattern seeker that continually attempts to cluster and organize information in keeping with previously formed synaptic structures (Caine, Caine, Klimek, & McClintic, 2008; Wolfe, 2010). Patterns are a way of making sense, of making meaning, of making connections to what we already know. This built-in tendency to look for patterns aids in young children's learning—in identifying colors and shapes, for example, and later in recognizing letters and words as early literacy skills develop.

We can capitalize on these pattern-seeking tendencies by teaching young children to compare how things are similar and different. A pig, a polar bear, and a tiger are similar in that they all have two eyes, two ears, one nose, one mouth, four legs, and a tail. But they are different in that a pig lives on a farm, a polar bear lives in the icy north, and a tiger lives in a jungle. Squares, triangles, and circles are all shapes, but a square has four sides, a triangle has three, and a circle has none; a rectangle is more like a square than either of the other two shapes. These are examples that are relevant in early childhood education and demonstrate the continued usefulness of comparison for older students in biology and geometry class. Research reported by Marzano (2007) indicates that students who receive explicit instruction about finding similarities and differences tend to do better academically in subjects like these than those who do not.

An early childhood teacher who points out that four pumpkins on a table are all orange is offering a basic lesson on identifying colors. By comparing the sizes, shapes, and different shades of orange ("Are some of these pumpkins a darker orange than others?"), the teacher and children take the activity to a more cognitive level, especially when they begin arranging the pumpkins by order of size or dividing them into groups of ovals and circles. And if the teacher asks young children to consider how this type of comparison and grouping might be useful in other situations, she is facilitating the transfer of developing cognitive skills.

Textbox 6.1. Learn With Us

The Story of Compo the Comparison Owl

Message: Comparing things is a good way to learn more about them.
Key words to introduce: compare, same, different

Many young animals live in the wilderness park, and each of them is really good at something. Everyone knows that if you need something from the top branches of the tree, you ask Giraffe. If you need something done fast, you ask Leopard. And if you need to solve problems, you ask Compo the Owl.

Compo is really good at comparing things. When you're good at comparing things, you can be really good at thinking, and people think you're smart. Compo shows Goat the best way to climb the mountain by comparing which paths have the best rocks for climbing. She shows Giraffe the best trees for eating by comparing which leaves are most tender. And she shows Gopher how to decide where to dig by comparing where the nicest soil is.

One day, Giraffe, Zebra, Tiger, and Leopard decide to play a game. But they can't decide how to choose teams and what to name their teams, so they ask Compo.

Compo looks at her animal friends. She thinks about what is the same and what is different about them. Giraffe has spots and a long, long neck. Zebra looks like a horse with stripes. Tiger and Leopard are both cats, but one has stripes and the other is spotted.

"I know!" Compo says. "Zebra and Tiger can be on one team. We'll call you Stripes. And Giraffe and Leopard can be on the other team. We'll call you Spots."

"Compo, you are so smart!" her animal friends tell her. "Go, Spots! Go, Stripes!"

"We can all be smart when we practice figuring out same and different," Compo says.

Activities: Make a game of sorting toys by comparing colors, shapes, and sizes. Sort toy animals into groups of farm animals and jungle animals or mammals, reptiles, fish, birds, and so on.

These stories are adapted with permission from the *Thinking for Reading Curriculum*, by Donna Wilson and Marcus Conyers (BrainSMART, 2005).

EARLY DRIVING LESSONS: STEERING YOUR BRAIN CAR

In earlier chapters, we described how infants and toddlers acquire increasingly complex motor and language skills. Parents proudly tick off every milestone their children achieve: first smile, first step, first word, first sentence, and those first painstaking attempts at reading and writing. What is just as noteworthy as any of these achievements—but not as easily recorded in a baby's keepsake memory book—is a child's progress toward self-regulation and self-control. Self-control is an important achievement of a developing brain. It's part of a cognitive processing system, known as **executive function**, which enables us to process the information we receive through our senses and then use that information to make decisions and solve problems.

Executive function is what allows individuals to inhibit inappropriate responses and to control impulses, but this is something that is not readily achieved by the immature brain of an infant or toddler. The prefrontal region matures more slowly than other parts of the brain (Giedd, n.d.). Thus, in young children, emotion and impulse often take precedent over cognitive reasoning. This lag in executive function is the reason that children's attention spans are shorter, why they throw tantrums when they don't get their way, and why they are more prone to crying in reaction to frustrating situations.

Self-regulation, inhibitory control, and **working memory** (the ability to remember information that may be important for immediate task completion and problem solving) are all important components of executive function. Executive function develops concurrently in the preschool years with **theory of mind** (ToM), the ability to predict or surmise how others might think and react in a certain situation based on one's own personal experience. There is evidence to suggest that the simultaneous emergence of executive function and theory of mind is not coincidental but rather related. Studies show that preschoolers' ability to complete tasks that are dependent on inhibitory control and working memory correlate strongly to ToM development (Carlson, Moses, & Breton, 2002).

Self-control starts as reflexive self-regulation in infancy, when babies self-soothe or avert their gaze to relieve discomfort and stress. It develops in toddlers to the point where they can communicate their needs and wants verbally and then progresses in early childhood as an ability to remember and follow rules (Blair, 2003). Like many developing skills, self-control can be taught and encouraged. Caring and attentive adults—both parents and early childhood educators—are in a position to work with children to help them develop more reasoned and appropriate responses in everyday situations. Whether it's learning to take turns during playtime or staying quiet when someone else is talking, every step a child takes toward better self-control is a step toward a better experience in academics and in life.

As authors and educators, we have developed a concept known as "driving your brain" (Wilson & Conyers, 2011b). Driving your brain is a lot like driving a car. In both cases, you need to have a clear idea of where you want to go. An important component of steering your brain efficiently is **metacognition**, which can be succinctly described as thinking about thinking with the aim of improving how you learn. By thinking about your thinking, you can identify which cognitive strategies work best for you and then adapt your methods of learning accordingly. For instance, perhaps you've found that you focus better after a morning run or that reading immediately before you go to bed does wonders for your retention. You may use a mnemonic device to remember simple facts like the colors of the rainbow or the names of the Great Lakes. You might make a habit of mentally running through checklists to ensure that you're completing every task you need to accomplish during the course of the day.

Kuhn (2000) suggests that the first steps toward metacognition emerge early in life (p. 178). As early as age 3, for example, children may be able to distinguish between thinking about an object and perceiving it, and they begin to talk about their own "thinking" and "knowing." By age 4, children seem to understand that people's beliefs and wants guide their behavior, that people's beliefs may differ, and that not all beliefs are correct. These are the first steps toward what Kuhn calls an important accomplishment—"people becoming aware of and reflective about their own thinking and able to monitor and manage the ways in which it is influenced by external sources, in . . . academic, work, and personal life settings" (p. 181).

Engaging With Educators

The children in Regina Cabadaidis's pre-K and kindergarten class will tell you precisely why Peter Rabbit was foolish enough to sneak into Mr. McGregor's vegetable patch and thus had to suffer the frightening consequences of running for his life and losing his brand-new clothes: The poor little bunny failed to use metacognition.

Ms. Cabadaidis introduced her students, who range in age from 3 to 6, to the concept of metacognition on the first day of school, writing the word in big letters on the white board at the front of the classroom.

"I explained to them that metacognition means 'thinking about your thinking,'" says Ms. Cabadaidis, who teaches at S. D. Spady Elementary School in Delray Beach, Florida. "We talk about metacognition all the time—why we need it and how it's important."

The children had this concept in mind on the day Ms. Cabadaidis read aloud The Tale of Peter Rabbit. When she got to the part of the story where Peter Rabbit disobeyed his mother and trespassed on Mr. McGregor's property, the children got very excited. As their teacher recalls, "They said, 'Peter Rabbit didn't have metacognition. He went into Mr. McGregor's farm when his mother told him not to, and he got into a lot of trouble. He lost the brass buttons to his new blue coat!'"

Ms. Cabadaidis reports that teaching her students to think about their thinking has been extremely effective in helping them develop self-control. "They're little, and they're still guided by their emotions. They're 3 to 6 years old, so sometimes an argument is instigated, and the children use their hands and feet to solve the disagreement. They're in 'brain-stem mode,' so it's important to tell them, 'Let's stop a minute and think about your thinking. You need to use your cognitive thinking skills. Think with your mind, and not with your hands and feet.'"

Driving your brain car becomes easier as metacognition improves. In their early years, however, children are essentially in the "passenger's seat" while adults make decisions about their lives. Not all of these decisions go down well with children. A parent may determine what food is placed before a toddler, but that doesn't mean the toddler will eat it. A teacher may ask her preschool class to stop talking and pay attention, but it doesn't necessarily follow that the children will adhere to those directions. Young children tend to follow their desires and impulses without consideration of consequences or other people's feelings. It is up to adults—the "driving instructors" in this analogy—to guide children to consider what will happen if they do not follow the desired course of action.

Let's look at three scenarios in which adults help young children take the first steps toward driving their brains.

Scenario 1

The situation. Three-year-old Brian refuses to eat the "yucky" chicken and vegetable casserole his mother has placed before him. She explains she spent a long time making this dinner because she wants him to eat something nutritious that will give him the energy to run and play. If Brian doesn't eat his dinner, he can't have dessert because that doesn't have the nutrition he needs. So, his mother makes a bargain. If he gives the casserole a try and still doesn't like it, she agrees to make him a peanut butter and jelly sandwich with grapes or carrot sticks on the side. However, he will not get dessert. The child mulls this over, decides to give the casserole a try, and finds out that it's not so bad. He eats enough of the casserole to "earn" the reward of a chocolate chip cookie for dessert.

Why this worked. Brian's mother is successful in steering her son to an acceptable solution by (a) emphasizing that she cares about him and his health, (b) making the connection between nutritious food and physical activity, (c) giving him a choice between two healthy meal alternatives, and (d) using a reward (the dessert) as a positive consequence for good behavior.

Scenario 2

The situation. Four-year-old Sarah loves to play with a lifelike baby doll in the play area of her preschool classroom. One day, she walks into the room and discovers a new girl cradling the doll in her arms. Angry and upset, Sarah rushes across the room and yanks the doll out of the hands of this unfamiliar child. The new girl bursts into tears, but Sarah is not deterred. She insists that this is "my doll" and that the new girl is not allowed to play with her. The preschool teacher intervenes, sits both girls down in chairs, hands out tissues, and then crouches down to talk to them in a calm, soothing voice. First of all, she explains to Sarah that, no matter how much she loves playing with the doll, all the toys belong to everyone in the classroom. Then, she explains the importance of sharing and taking turns. Finally, she introduces Sarah to Kimberly. She explains that Kimberly will need Sarah's help in finding other toys to play with when it is Sarah's turn to play with the doll. Soon, Sarah and Kimberly are exploring the toy box together, and Sarah happily gives Kimberly her turn with the doll as she rediscovers toys that she had completely forgotten about.

Why this worked. The preschool teacher diffuses an emotional situation and helps forge a positive relationship between Sarah and Kimberly by (a) empathizing with Sarah but calmly explaining the rules in a way that she can understand, (b) highlighting important concepts like sharing and taking turns that will allow the girls to practice self-control, (c) introducing the two girls to one another by name so that they relate to each other as peers, and (d) enlisting Sarah as a partner in helping Kimberly feel more comfortable in her new preschool setting.

Scenario 3

The situation. Mrs. Larson is having a hard time getting her preschool class to settle down once they come back inside after their 15-minute break on the playground. She knows that transitions between activities can be difficult, but today the children seem exceptionally rowdy. Several children are shouting, some are running around the room, and two are even wrestling and knocking over chairs. All of this noise and rough-housing is taking its toll on Mrs. Larson's patience and valuable learning time. Suddenly, she has an inspiration. She tells the children the class will be divided into teams, and they can choose the names of their teams themselves. The children agree on an animal theme, calling themselves the Krazy Koalas, the Laughing Lions, and the Friendly Frogs.

The change in the classroom atmosphere over the next few weeks is phenomenal. Mrs. Larson gives rewards to the first team that is seated and quietly drawing or reading immediately after playground time. Sometimes the reward entails letting the team pick out the storybook for reading time or letting them be first in line at the water table. Each team picks a different leader every week, and that child is responsible for making sure that his or her team follows the rules. The children feel happy, involved, and empowered, and Mrs. Larson has her patience back.

Why this worked. Mrs. Larson recognizes a problem in her classroom and solves it by (a) letting the kids participate in forming and naming teams, (b) putting the focus on following rules in which children practice self-control, (c) rotating the leadership roles so that the children can alternately give and get cooperation in their teams, and (d) using rewards as direct consequences of positive behavior.

What these three scenarios have in common is that the adults are modeling, encouraging, and rewarding self-control. They are calm, patient, resolute, and solution-driven. They devise methods to curb negative behavior and to help children recognize and reap the benefits of such positive behavior as decision making, sharing, empathizing, focusing their attention, and working together as a team. They are giving children excellent instruction that will enhance their ability to drive their brains.

Another common thread in these scenarios—and throughout this section—is that children benefit when adults provide *explicit* instruction on cognitive strategy use. As preschool administrator Cari Rotenberger suggests, "Teaching children *how* to learn often becomes more important than *what* they learn." In completing her graduate studies, Ms. Rotenberger, who is assistant director of the First Congregational Church Weekday Preschool and Kindergarten in Winter Park, Florida, conducted an action research project implementing developmentally appropriate activities that introduce 5-year-olds to developing their intent to learn, plan systematically, and learn from experience as part of an inquiry science lesson about birds. "My goal was to help them acquire the tools necessary to effectively gather, manage, and use information," Ms. Rotenberger told us. "When this is done, children become more aware of their thinking and begin to exhibit metacognitive behaviors."

RESEARCH ON THE ROLE OF SELF-CONTROL IN LEARNING

Many researchers have found self-control to be an important precursor to learning. Children are better able to take in information if they pay attention, resist distractions, and have a clear intent about what they want to achieve.

Galinsky (2010) links the concept of self-control to focus:

> For young children, researchers talk about being "alert" and about "orienting" (being able to position their attention in the right direction

to achieve what they want to achieve—think of a fourteen-month-old trying to get Cheerios onto a spoon in order to feed herself or himself). For older children and adults, focus includes those two aspects, plus being able to concentrate—that is, to remain alert and oriented for a period of time, bringing out other skills to bear on a project or task despite internal and external distractions. (p. 16)

The most widely quoted study on the subject of self-control in children is the famous marshmallow test, conducted more than 40 years ago by psychologist Walter Mischel. The purpose of the study was to test preschool-age children's ability to delay immediate gratification for increased benefits in the future. In the study, a researcher placed a marshmallow (or other treat) on a table in front of a child. The child was to be left in the room for 15 minutes but was told not to eat the marshmallow until the researcher returned to the room. If the child was able to wait successfully, he or she would be rewarded with a second marshmallow.

Delaying gratification is difficult in young children, but the Mischel study indicated that children have better success when they are given effective cognitive strategies, such as being told to focus on something other than the reward. The children who were able to wait the longest— in other words, those who showed the most self-control by denying themselves the instant gratification of the single marshmallow—went on to use better coping strategies during adolescence and to score higher on their SAT tests in comparison to the children who were less successful at waiting (Shoda, Mischel, & Peake, 1990).

A more recent study, this one involving eighth-grade students in Philadelphia, also showed a correlation between self-discipline assessments and academic performance. The study showed that the self-discipline scores were more predictive of the students' final GPAs than IQ scores and also were more positively correlated with school attendance, hours spent doing homework, and other effective study habits (Duckworth & Seligman, 2005).

Self-Control and Quality of Life

The role of self-control also is well documented in the ongoing Dunedin Multidisciplinary Health and Development Study, which has followed more than 1,000 children born within a year's time in the city of Dunedin, New Zealand. After 32 years, the study had a 96% retention rate (Moffitt et al., 2011). Based on observational and correlational analysis, the study showed that self-control assessments conducted at 3 years of age were an excellent predictor of a variety of quality-of-life factors in the participants' adult lives. Children who were evaluated as having lower self-control were more likely to suffer from health problems such as obesity, hypertension, and high cholesterol during adulthood. They were more likely to be struggling financially, to have alcohol or drug abuse problems, to be single parents, and to have a criminal record. In fact, crime conviction rates were 43% for the lowest fifth, based on measured self-control, compared to only 13% for the highest fifth.

The researchers found that many of these problems stemmed from poor decision making in adolescence, when a higher percentage of the children evaluated to have poor self-control had taken up smoking, had dropped out of school, and had become unplanned teenage parents.

A related study, which tracked British twins from their birth in 1994 and 1995, rated participants with the same observational method for self-control as used in the Dunedin study. The purpose was to extricate the influence of the child's genetic makeup, social class, and home life, and to single out self-control levels as a factor in the results. The results showed that, at age 5, the twin with the poorer rating in self-control was more likely to begin smoking at age 12, which is regarded as a precursor to health problems in adulthood, and also to engage in other antisocial behaviors.

Conclusions drawn from these two longitudinal studies included the suggestion that intervention addressing the issue of self-control at a young age would have a positive effect on societal costs later. In fact, Moffitt and colleagues pointed out that addressing the self-control issue would be a more effective target for change than other factors:

> Differences between children in self-control predicted their adult outcomes approximately as well as low intelligence and low social class origins, which are known to be extremely difficult to improve through intervention. . . . Early childhood intervention that enhances self-control is likely to bring a greater return on investment than harm reduction programs targeting adolescents alone. (p. 2697)

Self-Regulation as a Predictor of School Readiness

Researchers also have determined that promotion of self-regulation can spell the difference between school readiness and early school failure. Blair and Diamond (2008) found that such skills as mathematics knowl-

edge, letter knowledge, and phonemic awareness were all positively correlated with executive function ability in preschool and kindergarten.
Conversely, children with poor or impaired executive function were
found to have problems paying attention, completing assignments, and
inhibiting impulsive behaviors.

Children with good self-control and focus are likely to receive positive
reinforcement from the teacher and also more likely to perceive school as
fun. Contrast that to the experience of children who have poor self-control. Those children are less likely to learn and are more likely to be
caught in what Blair and Diamond (2008) described as a "negative feedback loop" that can lead to poor self-perception and lowered expectations
that can deter academic progress in the future. Fortunately, the researchers noted that there are examples of early childhood education programs
(Tools of the Mind and the Promoting Alternative Thinking Strategies
program, among them) that are helping children achieve better self-regulation skills. Their conclusion:

> A central goal for prekindergarten and early elementary education
> should be to develop curricula to promote self-regulation through in-
> structional and emotional support and to utilize well-developed and
> appropriate measures to assess the effects to these curricula on the
> development of social-emotional, cognitive, and early academic abil-
> ities. (p. 907)

Florez (2011) stressed that early childhood teachers can help young
children regulate their thinking and behavior through a variety of techniques. She observed:

> Helping children develop self-regulation skills is similar to helping
> children learn to read, count, or ride a bike. Effective teachers use a
> variety of strategies to bridge the developmental space between what
> children already know and can do and more complex skills and knowl-
> edge. (p. 49)

Instructional Strategies and Self-Regulation

Early childhood educators, parents, and caregivers can use a variety
of instructional strategies to promote self-regulation among children. Florez cited three effective methods:

- **Modeling.** Teachers demonstrate appropriate behavior and social skills, such as taking turns, inviting other children to participate in an activity, and sharing.
- **Hints and cues.** Teachers provide guidance by offering simple directions, making suggestions, gesturing or pointing to focus a child's attention, gently touching the shoulder or patting the back (as long as the child does not mind being touched), and commenting in a helpful manner.
- **Withdrawing adult support.** Teachers skillfully and gradually diminish their support so that children truly do become more self-regulating. This strategy reflects the concept of scaffolding, drawn from Vygotsky's work (1978) on how adults can guide children to hone their developing abilities and previously mentioned in Chapter 5.

Eventually, young children learn how to translate cues from adults to inhibit socially unacceptable impulses, such as grabbing toys or pushing past other children in line for an activity instead of waiting their turn. Just as they improve in their reading and writing skills, they also improve in self-regulation and self-control.

The AEIOU learning cycle can be an effective strategy for helping children to improve their self-control, as shown in Table 6.1. In classroom settings, the AEIOU model lends itself to discussions that can help preschoolers work on the issue of self-regulation together.

PRAISE EFFORT, NOT RESULTS

Expectations can have a powerful impact on school performance. Children get labeled—by themselves and others—as being "smart" or "dumb." These labels tend to stick, and poorer-performing children eventually may feel that there is no sense in fighting it. They begin to believe that they don't do well in school because they just aren't that bright.

Recent revelations about the plasticity of the brain (as described in Chapter 1) disprove the notion that intelligence is a fixed trait. Instead, as we have noted throughout this text, educational psychologists and researchers talk about the concept of **malleable intelligence**, which takes into account the ability to enhance cognitive development through experiences and environmental influences. We've already discussed many of

Table 6.1.   AEIOU in Action: Self-Control

A	Awareness	Storybook time is a favorite part of the day in this early childhood program, but a few children have a hard time staying quiet so that others can hear the teacher. Even these children acknowledge they are being too noisy, and they try to be quiet but soon fall into their old habits.
E	Exploration	After several admonitions, the teacher admits she is perplexed. Why is it so hard for children to be quiet and listen so that everyone can enjoy the story? Everyone ponders this question a moment. One boy says he just gets so excited about the story that he wants to talk about it right away. Another says that when children around her begin talking, it makes her want to talk, too.
I	Inquiry	The teacher asks the children if they can all work together to come up with a solution to the storybook time problem. They have been learning to "stop and think" when they encounter a problem, so everyone pauses to ponder. Then a child suggests that if someone has something to say or ask about the story, he or she should raise a hand. The teacher thinks this is worth a try, and the other children agree.
O	Order	The class tries out the new plan. But so many children are raising their hands so often that it's hard to get through the story. So the teacher suggests that she will stop at least three times in every story to ask if there are questions or comments. She reminds them all to listen very carefully to make sure they know what is happening in the story. The children agree to the new plan.
U	Understanding/ Use	At the next storybook session, the teacher picks out a brand-new book the class has never heard before. She reads the first part of the story and then stops to ask questions. What has happened so far? Why does the main character take the actions that he does? This results in a lively discussion in which the children tell about incidents from their own lives that are similar to what is occurring with the main character. The teacher quiets down the class to resume reading, and they listen in rapt attention to find out what happens next.

these influences in previous chapters, such as talking to children, reading aloud, and surrounding them with books; in this chapter, we add the importance of helping children develop self-control. Children are more likely to achieve their academic goals if they have learned how to wield self-control and maintain focus, if they receive encouragement from the adults in their life, and if they feel positive about their chances for success.

In the previous chapter, we told you about the Hart and Risley research that revealed a gap of 30 million words between the number heard by children in the highest socioeconomic groups and by those in the lowest. The differences in the types of verbal interactions researchers observed taking place in these families were also noteworthy. Based on recorded conversations, the study found that children in the highest socioeconomic group received an average of 32 affirmative statements and 5 prohibitory statements per hour, a positive ratio of 6 to 1. Children in the middle socioeconomic group received an average of 12 affirmatives and 7 prohibitions per hour, or an approximate positive ratio of 2 to 1.

In contrast, parents in the lowest socioeconomic group provided an average of 5 affirmative statements and 11 prohibitions an hour to their children, or a rounded ratio of 1 encouragement to 2 discouragements. None of these children were neglected, abused, or otherwise mistreated. However, the number of prohibitions added up. By the age of 4, the average child in the lowest socioeconomic group might have had 144,000 fewer encouraging interactions and 84,000 more prohibitive interactions than the average child in the middle socioeconomic group (Hart & Risley, 2003).

Distinguishing Different Kinds of Praise

Our previous discussions about practical optimism underscored the importance of a positive learning environment to support learning gains. As children start to have their first academic experiences as preschoolers, the praise they receive from their teachers, parents, and other adults becomes a direct means of communicating that they have the ability to do well. Murray and Fortinberry (2006) describe three kinds of praise:

- Praise for achievement (what children do) is the most obvious and frequently given kind of praise. "It's from the praise of others that a person gets a sense of competence. . . . The downside of achievement praise can be if it's the only kind given" (p. 100). Achievement praise should be specific and weighted. The authors use the example of the difference between finishing dinner and riding a bike for the first time; only one of those probably deserves a "That's fantastic!" The authors caution that indiscriminate praise "devalues the effort the child has put into learning a difficult new skill" (p. 100).

- Praise for process (how they do it), for persistent effort and inventiveness, is especially effective. "Process praise is not focused on outcomes, yet it helps children actually do better at tasks" (p. 101) because they learn that how they do something matters. This type of praise highlights learning progress and ultimate mastery (see Chapter 4).
- Praise for the person (who they are) is also important. "People need to know that they're valued just because of who they are, without having to strive for this recognition" (p. 102). At home and in early childhood programs, the aim should be to create positive environments where children feel safe, secure, valued, and encouraged to try new things. Recognizing children for their unique and positive attributes—for having an interesting idea, for helping a friend or teacher, for having a great laugh or a sunny smile—enhances their own good feelings about themselves and their abilities.

In the words of Seligman and colleagues (2007), young children thrive in an atmosphere where "love, affection, warmth and ebullience are delivered unconditionally" (p. 287) but where praise is provided contingent on success and in proportion to the accomplishment. Educational researchers and psychologists tend to agree on the critical distinction between praising children for their intelligence and praising them for their hard work and effort. As Galinsky (2010) explains:

> One of the main ways that we can change children's views about themselves and their world is by how we comment on their accomplishments or failures. Rather than praising their personalities or intelligence ("You are so smart" or "artistic" or "athletic"), criticizing them ("You are so stupid" or "uncoordinated"), or attributing their accomplishments to luck, we can praise their efforts or strategies. (p. 297)

Galinsky adds that children who receive praise for their effort rather than their intelligence are more willing to take risks, feel more comfortable in making mistakes, and are more likely to take on learning challenges that are hard but worthwhile. They're not afraid of trying something new and failing because they don't believe the outcome says something negative about their intelligence or ability.

Incremental vs. Fixed Intelligence

These findings are compatible with Dweck's work on "mindsets" (discussed in Chapter 4), which indicates that children work harder when they believe that intelligence is not a fixed trait but can be improved through hard work and access to learning opportunities. Dweck, together with colleagues Mangels and Good (2004), described how different perceptions of intelligence have an influence:

> When students believe that their intelligence is a fixed trait (an entity theory of intelligence), it becomes critical for them to validate their fixed ability through their performance. In contrast, when students believe that their intellectual skills are something that they can increase through their efforts (an incremental theory of intelligence), they become less concerned with how their abilities might be evaluated now, and more concerned with cultivating their abilities in the longer term. (p. 42)

This conceptualization shows that the type of praise adults offer children can play an important role in how children view their own intelligence and learning opportunities. A series of studies involving school-age children found that praise for intelligence had more negative consequences on the students' achievement motivation than praise for effort (Mueller & Dweck, 1998). Students praised for intelligence were found to care more about performance goals, whereas students praised for their effort were found to be more interested in pursuing activities that promised increased learning. Moreover, students previously praised for intelligence reacted more poorly to a test failure than those who had previously been praised for effort in that they showed less task persistence and less task enjoyment and did worse at task performance than they did prior to the failure. Mueller and Dweck observed that effort-related praise may lead children to understand that there is a correlation between hard work and the possibilities for learning and improvement:

> Children praised for their hard work may learn to attribute their performance to effort, which can vary in amount, rather than to a stable ability. Thus they will interpret subsequent poor performance as indicating a temporary lapse in effort rather than as a deficit in intelligence. (p. 34)

Medina (2010) likewise noted that praising for intelligence can eventually be detrimental. All is well and good, so long as the child is performing well in school, but what happens if the child hits a rough patch and suddenly is having difficulty? The child will perceive such setbacks as failures:

> Because you told her that success was due to some static ability over which she had no control, she will start to think of failure (such as a bad grade) as a static thing, too—now perceived as a lack of ability. Successes are thought of as gifts rather than the governable product of effort. (p. 140)

Praise is best when it refers to something specific and also when it targets something under the child's control (Aamodt & Wang, 2011). Effort-related praise accomplishes both of these criteria. When you praise children for their hard work, you are reinforcing their behavior and making it more likely that they will continue to work hard to keep praise coming in the future. Eventually, the positive results produced by their hard work will serve as just as large, or even larger, a motivator than the praise they receive from others. They will have internalized the reward; praise, while nice, will no longer be a prerequisite for continuing to put forth an effort to achieve their learning goals.

AN EARLY START TO LIFELONG LEARNING

Through the first six chapters of this book, we have stressed the importance of establishing a strong foundation for young children during the first five critical years in life. Offering young children many opportunities and encouragement to explore new things and make steady progress on their skills and abilities in a positive learning environment sets them on a path to flourish now and in the future. Ramey and Ramey (1999) offer "seven essentials" for adults who work with young children as a means to set them on a positive path for lifelong learning.

1. **Encourage.** Encourage children to explore their world safely, using all their senses in a variety of places, alone and with others.
2. **Mentor.** Mentor in basic skills, showing the whats and whens, the ins and outs of how things and people work.
3. **Celebrate.** Celebrate developmental advances, such as learning new skills and becoming a unique individual.

4. **Rehearse.** Rehearse and extend new skills, showing how to practice again and again, in the same and different ways, with new people and new things.
5. **Protect.** Protect children from inappropriate disapproval, teasing, neglect, or punishment.
6. **Communicate.** Communicate often and responsively with sounds, songs, gestures, and words.
7. **Guide.** Guide and limit behavior to keep children safe and teach them what is acceptable and what is not.

☆*PRACTICAL TIPS FOR EARLY CHILDHOOD EDUCATORS*☆

Cultivating Problem Solving and Development of Self-Control

Model and accentuate problem solving. As the lead learner, take advantage of opportunities to demonstrate and talk through problem-solving situations, and invite children to share and try out possible solutions. For example, "these new blocks are so much fun that everyone wants to play with them. How can we solve this problem and make sure that everyone who wants to gets a turn?" And be sure to celebrate successful solutions: "It was great how you helped Sarah search for and find her missing mitten. Great problem solving to look under the boot bench!"

Engage the senses in learning activities. Guide children to make meaning of new concepts through activities that involve listening and talking with adults and other children, getting involved through hands-on learning and experimenting, and using as many senses as possible. For example, the sense of smell plays a role in triggering memories, so while you're planting a garden, encourage children to smell the dirt, to see if the bulbs and seeds they are planting have a smell, and, of course, to smell the flowers, fruits, and vegetables that come from gardens!

Put the brain's pattern-seeking proclivities to work. Like Compo the Comparison Owl (see Textbox 6.1), young children will benefit from looking at how things are the same and different. Color coding is a great way to accentuate patterns and grouping, such as storing toys and art supplies for each learning center in the same color bins. You can seek out patterns in nature, such as looking for different shapes while on a walk in the park (acorns are round, some leaves look like triangles, and the planks on a walking path are shaped like rectangles). Animal toys and pictures can be grouped by various attributes, including size, species, and habitat.

Emphasize self-control and positive feedback. Adults can provide children with opportunities to practice self-control throughout their everyday experiences (Florez, 2011). Likewise, offering positive feedback can be a part of daily activities. Here are a few suggestions for helping children develop self-control and giving them feedback in a constructive and helpful way:

- Provide age-appropriate learning experiences. Keep in mind that self-control is a progression in the developing young mind. Avoid criticizing a young child's inability to sit still for a long lesson. It's simply not yet within his or her skill range. As Blair and Diamond (2008) note: "Young children need to be actively doing. They can learn cognitive and emotional regulation skills, and academic content, best through actively participating in activities, including structured play."

- Plan activities. Planning is an important part of self-regulation (Florez, 2011). As an early childhood educator, work out a schedule for your students that is predictable and helps establish a routine. That doesn't mean the day has to be boring. Let children choose what books are going to be read during story time or what types of activities they'll be doing during playtime. With a variety of books and toys available, children will enjoy being able to contribute to the makeup of their day.

- Play games. Games are an excellent way to familiarize children with the concept of playing by the rules and taking turns. Aamodt and Wang (2011)observed that board games can teach children to curb their negative impulses, such as moving when it's not their turn. Children sometimes have a difficult time when they lose or when the game is too complicated. Be sure to pick age-appropriate games of short duration with an element of luck so that they can be played multiple times to produce a variety of winners. Celebrate each child's victory with applause all around.

- Praise judiciously. Positive feedback is a way to help children develop their sense of self-worth, but it can also be a bit of a quagmire. As Johnston (2012) observes, if you praise one child with "good" and another child with "excellent," then suddenly "good" isn't good enough as a compliment. Johnston adds that process-oriented praise can be effective ("I like the way you did *x*"), though he cautions against turning praise into the point of the child's activities. This might take their focus away from what they are doing and turn it toward trying to please you. Sometimes, showing real interest in a child's work is more beneficial than trying to work in words of praise.

SEVEN

Addressing Risks to Healthy Development

The first six chapters of this text describe the optimal conditions that allow children to flourish in their first five years of life. We've discussed the importance of talking with children, reading to them, modeling optimism, praising their efforts, providing opportunities to puzzle through problems and come up with their own meaningful solutions, and helping them develop self-control so they can achieve more in their lives. The common denominator in all of these endeavors is the presence of caring, supportive adults—parents and knowledgeable early childhood educators, child-care professionals, community leaders, school administrators, and others—all of whom are collectively focused on helping children make the most of their learning opportunities. Our goal in this chapter is to examine some risks to healthy development in early childhood and to discuss how all these caring adults can work together to ensure that all children, even those facing neurobiological and/or environmental challenges, receive the support they need to fulfill their potential to learn, to progress, and to succeed.

Unfortunately, many children do not face optimal conditions in their lives. Some are born into poverty or have a home life troubled by violence, abuse, or neglect. Still others have physical or mental disabilities, conditions that in some cases could have been avoided if their mothers had had adequate prenatal care or fully understood the dangers of drinking alcohol and smoking during pregnancy.

Consider the following sobering statistics that detail the risks that confront the United States' youngest citizens:

- Of babies born in the United States in 2011, 8.1% had **low birth weights** (defined as less than 2,500 grams or approximately 5½ pounds), which put them at higher risk for disabilities and death (Hamilton, Martin, & Ventura, 2012).
- Pregnant women who receive late (third trimester) or no prenatal care are more likely to have babies with health problems. Those who receive no prenatal care are 3 times more likely to give birth to a baby with low birth weight; it is 5 times more likely their baby will die (Child Trends Data Bank, 2012).
- Fourteen million American children live in families with incomes below the federal poverty level, and more than 29 million children live in low-income households (Wright, Chau, & Aratani, 2010).
- "Food insecurity" is experienced by 20.6% of U.S. households with children, meaning that individuals in these 8 million homes don't always have access to sufficient food required for a healthy, active life. In nearly 4 million of those households in 2011, the children themselves experienced food insecurity on one or more occasions (Coleman-Jensen, Nord, Andres, & Carlson, 2012).
- An estimated 3.4 million reports of child abuse and neglect were received by Child Protective Services (CPS) in 2011. More than 676,000 children—a rate of 9.1 per 1,000—were confirmed as victims. Children in the age group of birth to 1 year had the highest rate of victimization at 21.2 per 1,000 children (U.S. Department of Health and Human Services, 2012).
- In 2011, the birth rate among 15- to 19-year-olds in the United States was 31.3 births per 1,000 women, down significantly from the 41.5 rate per 1,000 in 2007 (Hamilton et al., 2012). However, this rate is still more than double the teen pregnancy rates in many other developed countries, such as Switzerland, Japan, the Netherlands, Sweden, Italy, France, Norway, Finland, Germany, and Canada (United Nations, 2011).

Several risk factors occur during fetal development and early childhood and threaten healthy development, among them the following:

- maternal alcohol use during pregnancy;
- fetal exposure to smoking;

- low birth weight and undernutrition;
- genetic disorders;
- violence, abuse, and neglect;
- poverty;
- stress and depression; and
- teen pregnancy.

Unabated, these risk factors can have a substantial negative impact on brain development during critical periods of synaptogenesis as described in Chapter 1. However, the encouraging news is that risk does not equate with destiny. Preventative measures can be undertaken to help children mitigate or overcome the detrimental effects of early childhood stress and developmental challenges.

In our book *Courageous Learners* (Wilson & Conyers, 2010), we define four forces for increasing achievement among children who face environmental and/or neurobiological challenges: (1) professional development of educators, (2) parental support, (3) community involvement, and (4) early childhood education. The impact of these forces is a theme that underlies this text. Specifically, we believe that educating parents, caregivers, and teachers of young children about brain-based learning is the best way to ensure that toddlers and preschoolers grow up in an enriched environment that supports healthy cognitive, emotional, social, and physical development. Just because young children face risks and challenges does not mean they are doomed to a life where they cannot learn.

In the remainder of this chapter, we will provide a realistic assessment of the risks to development but also offer hopeful signs and courses of action that caring professionals can take to help young children move beyond these risks and realize their full potential for learning and flourishing. Our aim in this discussion of the risk factors in healthy child development is not to paint a bleak picture for the future of our youth. Rather, we seek to identify the challenges facing parents and other family members, early childhood educators, health professionals, and policy makers in making sure children have every opportunity to grow and thrive in safe, supportive environments.

SOURCES OF TOXIC STRESS AND ITS IMPACT ON LEARNING

Many of the risk factors cited previously—including violence, abuse, neglect, and poverty—are correlated with what is known as **toxic stress**, which the National Scientific Council on the Developing Child (2005) defines as "strong, frequent, or prolonged activation of the body's stress management system," brought about by stress events in the child's life that are "chronic, uncontrollable, and/or experienced without the child having access to support from caring adults" (p. 1).

The National Scientific Council also identifies lesser and even beneficial forms of stress. **Positive stress**, characterized by mild elevation of heart rate and stress hormone levels, occurs as a part of everyday life and is considered necessary for healthy development. Trigger events for a child to experience positive stress might be meeting someone new, adjusting to a new child-care setting, or overcoming a fear of animals. Optimally, the child would have a caring adult nearby during these experiences to serve as a calming influence and to explain that the stress reactions are normal.

Tolerable stress is a more severe form of stress that occurs during a major event in the child's life, such as the death or serious illness of a loved one, parental divorce or separation, or an accidental injury. While all of these events are difficult for the child to experience, they are made more manageable when the child is supported by caring adults who can help him or her cope and recover.

However, the unrelenting nature of toxic stress has the potential for being truly detrimental to a child's well-being. The prolonged elevation of **cortisol** levels (cortisol is a steroid hormone released in the brain in response to stress) that occurs during constant stress can be disruptive to the child's development and make him or her much more vulnerable to a range of behavioral and physiological orders throughout life, as the National Scientific Council describes:

> Studies indicate that such stress responses can have an adverse impact on brain architecture. In the extreme, such as in the cases of severe, chronic abuse, toxic stress may result in the development of a smaller brain. Less extreme exposure to toxic stress can change the stress system so that it responds at lower thresholds to events that might not be stressful to others, thereby increasing the risk of stress-related physical and mental illness. (p. 1)

Risk factors such as child abuse or neglect, parental substance abuse, and maternal depression are the types of stressors that are likely to induce a toxic stress response. Shonkoff and colleagues (2012) observed that the occurrence of these stressors at pivotal stages in childhood development could lead to serious deficiencies in cognitive and linguistic skills, memory, and various aspects of executive functioning:

> The essential characteristic of this phenomenon is the postulated disruption of brain circuitry and other organ and metabolic systems during sensitive developmental periods. Such disruption may result in anatomic changes and/or physiologic dysregulations that are the precursors of later impairments in learning and behavior as well as the roots of chronic, stress-related physical and mental illness. (p. e236)

Shonkoff and colleagues associated prolonged stress of this nature with a weak foundation for later learning and good health. These associations are supported by the findings of the widely cited Adverse Childhood Experiences Study, which correlated adverse conditions in childhood (e.g., abuse, neglect, parental substance abuse) with adverse health conditions in adulthood, ranging from higher incidences of heart disease, emphysema, and cancer to greater likelihood of smoking, alcoholism, drug abuse, poverty, and depression. Multiple adverse experiences were found to have a cumulative effect. For instance, those who had four or more adverse experiences in childhood were twice as likely to be smokers when reaching adulthood, 7 times more likely to suffer from alcoholism, and nearly 5 times more likely to have used illicit drugs (Anda et al., 2006).

Violence, Abuse, and Neglect in the Home Environment

As described previously, children experience toxic stress when raised in a violent, abusive environment over which they have no control. When trapped in such an environment, children are at risk of not only stress but also emotional maltreatment, serious injury, and even death. Policy research by Daro (2010) analyzed the Federal National Incidence Study on Child Maltreatment (NIS 4), which amasses data on reported child abuse and neglect nationwide. The NIS 4 reported a 19% reduction in the rate of child maltreatment since 1993 in the areas of sexual abuse, physical abuse, and emotional abuse. However, no significant changes were seen in the rate of child neglect; in fact, reports of emotional neglect, which includes parents' inattention to their children's development or behaviors, increased 83% over this period. Overall, Daro reports, the rate of children harmed as well as those who could be in danger of harm because of abuse or neglect remains a significant problem.

The problem of abuse and neglect is especially critical in our nation's cities. The leading cause of mortality among pregnant women and those within a year of childbirth in many urban areas is homicide. Infants born to women in violent home settings have higher rates of low birth weight and prematurity and are more likely not to gain weight and flourish in comparison to infants removed from violent settings (Feerick & Silverman, 2006).

Children whose needs are neglected face myriad risks, including malnutrition, injury or death by accident, and lagging cognitive development. The rate of death by accidental injury among young children has fallen dramatically in recent years, but accidents such as suffocation, motor vehicle collisions, and drowning remain the leading cause of death among infants and toddlers (Safe Kids USA, 2008).

Child psychiatrist Bruce Perry (2007, with Szalavitz) suggests that early childhood experiences that involve violence, threat, or significant stress in effect "rewire" the brain. To survive, the brain develops more receptor sites for noradrenaline, which leads to behaviors that may include overarousal, strong attention to nonverbal cues, and aggressiveness. The area of the brain responsible for emotions and positive attachments tends to be 20% to 30% smaller in abused children than those raised in nonabusive environments (Conkling, 2001).

Any adult who knows or suspects that a child is being neglected or is living in a violent, abusive home has an absolute obligation to report such behavior to the Child Protective Services agency in their area. Intervention is essential to stop this detrimental behavior as early as possible so that the child has the opportunity to experience a secure and safe environment, ideally with a nonabusive parent or other caring adult family members.

Benefits of Early Intervention

Stopping the risk at an early age is key. As we noted at the outset of this chapter, a child's exposure to risk factors does not make poor developmental outcomes a foregone conclusion. Detrimental factors that cause toxic stress can be mitigated by a stable environment that provides young children with consistent, nurturing, and protective interactions with adults (Shonkoff et al., 2012).

Timely intervention can also mean that potential damage experienced early in life can be reversed. Just as it is possible to help children recover emotionally from abuse and neglect, the neuroplasticity of the infant and toddler brain also means that young children may recover from brain injury as a result of accident or abuse. In a study of preschool children with a wide variety of brain injuries suffered before their first birthday, researchers found that cognitive deficits were milder than those observed in brain-injured adults. By age 5, virtually all impairments had disappeared. The perceptual, cognitive, and motor experiences those children had as they recovered from injury stimulated intact areas of the cerebral cortex to compensate for the early damage (Berk, 2001).

Similarly, the National Scientific Council on the Developing Child (2005) observes that there is no scientific evidence to support the view that young children exposed to significant early stress in life will always develop stress-related disorders. In fact, studies involving young animals after infancy show the opposite, wherein exposure to environments rich in opportunities for exploration and social play compensated in part for the negative behavioral consequences of prenatal stress and postnatal neglect.

Ultimately, relationships with caring adults provide intervention that allows children to deal with stress in a more positive manner:

> The relationships children have with their caregivers play critical roles in regulating stress hormone production during the early years of life. Those who experience the benefits of secure relationships have a more controlled stress hormone reaction when they are upset or frightened. This means that they are able to explore the world, meet challenges, and be frightened at times without sustaining the adverse neurological impacts of chronically elevated levels of hormones such as cortisol that increase reactivity of selected brain systems to stress and threat. (National Scientific Council on the Developing Child, 2005, p. 3)

In addition, the quality of early childhood care and education is an important component in reducing children's stress levels. This conclusion is supported by a study that found significant increases in cortisol in children in low-quality child-care settings but not in children who were in high-quality care settings (Geoffroy, Coté, Parent, & Seguin, 2006). In contrast to low-quality child-care settings, high-quality environments are characterized by more personalized care, better trained caregivers, a greater emphasis on educational play, and more positive peer interaction—factors that appear to correlate with less stress and more positive experiences for children.

Conditions Related to Learning Challenges

Millions of children face learning challenges that are not overcome by changing their home environments. Conditions such as **Down syndrome, attention deficit hyperactivity disorder (ADHD), autism, fetal alcohol syndrome,** and low birth weight are caused by genetics, biological conditions, and environmental factors. While these are lifelong conditions, the support of parents, educators, school administrators, and community program professionals can make the difference in children achieving the fullest extent of their potential in school and in life.

Genetic Disorders

Genes are molecules of deoxyribonucleic acid (**DNA**) and protein. DNA is the principal component of living tissue that contains the genetic code responsible for the inheritance and transmission of chromosomes and genes. Each cell contains the human genome, a string of 3 billion markers labeled by geneticists with the letters *A*, *C*, *G*, and *T*. The sequence, which spells out a complete set of instructions for making a human being, is almost identical in each one of the 100 trillion cells in the human body.

Genes are units of heredity passed from parents to offspring and are contained in cells. Every human cell contains 20,000 to 25,000 genes. Each microscopic cell contains about 6 feet of DNA thread—that's a total of 3 billion miles of DNA inside each body. Normally, every cell in the body (except for sperm and egg cells) has 46 chromosomes in 23 pairs. There are 22 nonsex chromosome pairs, called autosomes, and one sex chromosome pair (the male pair is XY, and the female pair is XX).

Heritability is the degree to which a characteristic is determined by a person's genes. Genetic disorders are diseases or disorders caused by gene mutation or chromosomal defects. Torpy, Lynm, and Glass (2008) classify genetic disorders in three general categories:

1. **Monogenetic disorders** are caused by a mutation in a single gene. The mutation is inherited from parents and may be present on one or both chromosomes. In some cases, children are born with an unexpected genetic disorder that no known family member has or has had before. Examples include sickle cell anemia, cystic fibrosis, polycystic kidney disease, and Tay-Sachs disease.

2. **Chromosome disorders** are characterized by an abnormal number of chromosomes; children may have more or fewer than the typical 46 chromosomes. For example, children with Down syndrome have an extra copy of chromosome 21.
3. Several different genes, sometimes in combination with environmental factors, can cause multifactorial diseases such as asthma and diabetes.

Just what role genetics plays in certain disorders is not fully understood. In the case of autism, the Autism Society (n.d.) observed that researchers have discovered that other factors beyond the genetic component might contribute to the disorder, including environmental toxins such as heavy metals. A recent study from the Centers for Disease Control and Prevention (CDC, 2012a) identifies an estimated 1 in 88 children in the United States as having an autism spectrum disorder (ASD). With such a high rate of occurrence, the Interagency Autism Coordinating Committee (IACC) at the U.S. Department of Health and Human Services is addressing the need for ASD research, screening, intervention, and education. Key to this effort will be improving the percentage of early diagnoses. The CDC study revealed that 40% of children are not diagnosed with ASD until after the age of 4. The good news, however, is that diagnoses before the age of 3 have increased from 12% for children born in 1994 to 18% for those born in 2000. Early diagnosis leads to early intervention and the ability to place children in preschool programs that will address their specific needs.

ADHD also is believed to have a strong genetic component due to its high rate of heritability (Faraone et al., 2005). A neurobehavioral disorder that is characterized by pervasive inattention, hyperactivity, and impulsivity, ADHD is the most commonly diagnosed neurobehavioral disorder among children, with parent-reported cases at 9.5% of children ages 4 to 17 in 2007, a total of 5.4 million (CDC, 2010).

Guralnick (2005) stresses the importance of early intervention in addressing intellectual disabilities, whether such disabilities have arisen from genetic and infectious causes, from biological conditions (such as malnutrition, head injuries, lead poisoning, and low birth weight), or from environmental causes (including poverty, child abuse, and neglect). He pinpoints the first 5 years of life as a critical period for systematic and comprehensive intervention, noting:

It is anticipated that early intervention will enhance the development of young children already exhibiting intellectual delays . . . both by altering their developmental trajectories and by preventing secondary complications from occurring. For children at risk of intellectual delays because of a variety of biological and/or environmental conditions, it is expected that the delays can be prevented entirely or their magnitude minimized. (p. 314)

Early intervention programs have the added benefit of identifying and mitigating stressors that are likely to have an impact on family members as they undertake the complex task of educating themselves about their child's condition as well grappling with the financial and emotional toll that it exacts. In an earlier work (1998), Guralnick stresses three key components of early intervention programs:

1. resource supports (awareness of, access to, and primary coordination of services, as well as supplemental supports such as financial assistance and respite care);
2. social supports (parent-to-parent groups, family counseling, and mobilization of family, friend, and community networks); and
3. information and services (such as a formal intervention program, either home or center-based; parent–professional relationships to address health and safety issues, to provide guidance, and to facilitate problem-solving; and individual therapies).

Prenatal Exposure to Stress, Alcohol, and Tobacco

Even before they are born, children can be put at risk by the behaviors and environmental conditions of their mothers during pregnancy. Maternal stress can be detrimental to normal fetal development, depending on its duration, intensity, timing, and cause. However, postnatal therapeutic interventions that put emphasis on parent–infant bonding and establishing an enriched environment can be largely effective in reversing the effects of prenatal stress, especially during the first year of life (Buss, Entringer, Swason, & Wadhwa, 2012).

While maternal stress is not always within the control of the mother-to-be, use of alcohol during pregnancy is something that can be controlled now that the risks are widely known. Tragically, however, tens of thousands of children suffer from the ill effects of alcohol absorption that occurred during fetal development. In monitoring the incidence of alcohol use among women of childbearing age from 2006 to 2010, the CDC (2012b) found that 1 in 13 pregnant women (7.6%) and more than half of nonpregnant women (51.5%) had reported drinking alcohol in the past 30 days; 1 in 71 (1.4%) pregnant women and 1 in 7 (15%) nonpregnant women had reported binge drinking during that same time period.

The prevalence of such alcohol use takes its toll every year. According to statistics from the National Organization on Fetal Alcohol Syndrome (NOFAS, 2012), fetal alcohol syndrome (FAS) or fetal alcohol spectrum disorders (FASD) are diagnosed in an estimated 40,000 babies born each year—or 1 in every 100 live births. As such, alcohol use during pregnancy is the single most preventable cause of birth defects, developmental disabilities, and learning disabilities. NOFAS stresses that there is no safe amount or type of alcohol that can be consumed at any time during pregnancy. Since developing babies are unable to process alcohol through the liver, they absorb all of the alcohol with potentially devastating consequences. In fact, alcohol causes more neurobehavioral damage in utero than heroin or cocaine.

Among the characteristics of FASD are distinctive facial features; low birth weight and other growth deficits; mild to severe brain damage; physical defects such as problems with the heart, lungs, or kidneys; behavioral or cognitive deficits; learning disabilities; speech and language delays; impaired thinking; diminished impulse control; emotional volatility; and poor social skills (National Organization on Fetal Alcohol Syndrome–South Dakota, 2009).

Another risk to fetal development—smoking tobacco during pregnancy—has been identified as the single largest modifiable risk factor for low birth weight and infant mortality. The CDC (2009) reports that babies born to women who smoke while pregnant have about 30% higher risk of being born prematurely and are more likely to be born with low birth weight. They are also about 1½ to 3 times more likely to die of sudden infant death syndrome (SIDS).

Smoking during pregnancy exposes the unborn baby to dangerous chemicals such as nicotine, carbon monoxide, and tar. As a result, babies receive less oxygen at a time when they need it for healthy growth and development. In addition, women who smoke during pregnancy are at greater risk of having an ectopic pregnancy, placenta previa, or a stillbirth. Babies are more likely to have birth defects, such as cleft lip or palate, or to suffer from conditions such as cerebral palsy or learning disabilities (March of Dimes, 2010).

Stages of Gestational Development

The effects of alcohol and tobacco use during pregnancy can be devastating due to the tremendous amount of growth and change that occurs during fetal development. Consider the following six major development effects that encompass the maturation of the **central nervous system**, including the brain and spinal cord (Aylward, 1997):

1. At 3 to 4 weeks gestation, a neural tube of neurons and glial cells is formed. The inner layer of this neural tube becomes the brain and spinal cord, and the outer layer becomes the skin.
2. At 5 to 6 weeks gestation, the **cerebrum** (the largest of the three major parts of the brain) and the face of the baby are formed.
3. Between 2 and 4 months gestation, about 200 billion neuroblasts (beginning of neurons) are produced to create the final 100 billion neurons that make up the brain.
4. Between 3 and 5 months, the neurons move (migrate) from their site of origin to their final position.
5. Between 6 months gestation and 5 years after birth, the neurons differentiate into their specific jobs by making connections (synapses). Synapses are overproduced in early development—up to 2 to 3 years old—and over time the neurons without connections are eliminated.
6. From 6 months gestation to adulthood, glial cells produce **myelin**, a fatty sheath that eventually covers and insulates axons to provide for rapid and efficient impulse transmission.

Considering these developmental events, it's essential to get the word out to mothers-to-be and potential mothers-to-be: If you think you might be pregnant or could become pregnant, don't drink or smoke. Prospective fathers also should not smoke to avoid the potential damage to the fetus from secondhand smoke.

In addition to the human toll of drinking and smoking during pregnancy, there is an economic toll as well. For instance, Dr. Larry Burd, director of the Fetal Alcohol Center at the University of North Dakota School of Medicine, estimates that the lifetime cost of caring for a child diagnosed with FAS is $3 million. He adds, "If starting today, no pregnant woman would ever take another drink, FAS would disappear. There'd never be another FAS baby, ever. Doesn't that make you stop and think?" (Stewart, 2005, p. 27).

Intervening on Behalf of Children with FASD

We have stressed repeatedly the importance of early intervention. To illustrate this point more clearly, let's explore how addressing an issue such as fetal alcohol syndrome or fetal alcohol spectrum disorders with specialized attention and education can be beneficial to the child. Many of these same principles can apply to children with other forms of learning challenges.

The National Organization on Fetal Alcohol Syndrome–South Dakota (NOFAS-SD) at the Center for Disabilities has prepared a handbook (2009) that enumerates education strategies for children with FASD. The handbook stresses the importance of a team approach, noting that a successful collaboration will involve not only parents, teachers, and students themselves but also school administrators and community service providers who specialize in mental health, social services, and developmental disabilities. The handbook lists five key strategies for working successfully with children with FASD:

1. Structure. Since children with FASD lack internal structure, parents, educators, and caretakers need to provide as much external structure as possible.
2. Consistency. Children with FASD need to have a sense that their surroundings are predictable. Thus, it is important for parents and educators to be consistent in their responses and daily routines.
3. Variety. Because children with FASD have deficiencies in executive function, parents and educators should use variety as a way of getting and maintaining their attention.
4. Brevity. Again because of lack of attention among children with FASD, it's important that parents and educators be brief with their instructions and explanations.
5. Persistence. Because cognitive skills are also compromised in children with FASD, repetition and persistent effort may be needed to guide them to achieve a successful learning experience.

The handbook stresses the importance of multisensory teaching methods that combine visual, auditory, and kinesthetic-tactile techniques to enhance memory and learning in children with FASD. Combining verbal instruction with visuals (such as illustrations, videos, and demonstrations) as well as using role-playing and field trips are ways to engage children and provide a more effective learning experience. As the NOFAS-SD reports:

> The most important thing to remember when teaching a student with an FASD is that the student has the capability to learn. Educators must work hard to find a way to assist the student with an FASD in discovering what helps him/her to learn and to enjoy the learning process. Educators must assist students with an FASD in becoming prepared for living the rest of their lives and working to their potential. (p. 13)

Impact of Low Birth Weight and Undernutrition

Another risk that is in many cases preventable is low birth weight, used to describe infants who weigh less than 5½ pounds at birth, and **preterm birth**, which describes infants who are born at less than 37 weeks gestation. As a result of advances in neonatal care, infants who weigh less than 2 pounds and are born at 23 weeks gestation may survive, but the risk of death and medical complications remains high for infants who are born too soon or too small. Low birth-weight infants have higher rates of subnormal growth, adverse health conditions, and developmental problems. Babies who are born 8 or more weeks early remain at high risk for mental and neurological problems, including visual, hearing, and motor deficits; poor emotional regulation; attention problems; and language delays. By elementary school age, children who weighed less than 3 pounds, 5 ounces at birth perform more poorly in school and score about 6 points lower on IQ tests than children born full term (Eliot, 1999).

Neonatal specialists are working to develop treatment to ensure the best possible outcomes for low birth weight and preterm infants. Guralnick (2012) reports promise in early intervention strategies that use high-quality parent–child transactions as their central component. Quality child-care or preschool programs are potentially another important element for these at-risk children; such programs can improve school readiness and enhance child competence in a way that contributes to higher-quality interactions between parents and children.

Premature infants with learning delays may benefit from more repetitive play to support brain development (Tracey & Maroney, 1999). Most healthy preterm infants catch up to their full-term peers in intellectual ability by 2 or 3 years of age because the brain can reorganize the brain connections and even rebuild damaged neural networks.

As we noted in Chapter 3, it's important that mothers-to-be eat well during pregnancy because a highly sensitive period of brain development begins around midway through gestation. Good nutrition during pregnancy and the first few years of life is a vital component for ensuring healthy synaptic development. Pregnant women have an obligation to their unborn children to obtain prenatal care that includes proper nutritional guidance to minimize the risks that result from low birth weight. Early interventions may mitigate the risks for preterm and low birthweight newborns, but the best intervention of all comes from parents-to-be who do whatever they can to maximize the possibility of giving birth to a full-term baby at a healthy weight.

ADDRESSING THE LINKS BETWEEN POVERTY AND SCHOOL READINESS

A child is born into poverty every 33 seconds in the United States, according to *The State of America's Children*, a 2010 report from the Children's Defense Fund. From 2000 to 2007, poverty increased by 1.7 million children for a total of 13.3 million children living in poverty. One in 3 Latino children and 3 in 7 African American children are born into poverty. One in 12 children lives in extreme poverty, which means their families survive on half or less the annual poverty level of $22,050 for a family of four. Economic deprivation affects the parents' and children's nutrition, access to medical care, safety, level of stress, and quality of child care. More than half of all poor children live in eight states: California, Texas, New York, Florida, Illinois, Georgia, Ohio, and Michigan.

Family income level is closely linked to academic performance (Rampell, 2009), most likely because of the spiraling effects of the benefits of higher education. That is, college graduates earn more than people whose education stops at high school; they understand the value of a good education and encourage their own children to do well in school. This support and encouragement begins early in life. In low-income households, on the other hand, "parents who are preoccupied with a daily struggle to ensure that their children have enough to eat and are safe from harm may not have the resources, information, or time they need to provide the stimulating experiences that foster optimal brain development" (Hawley, 2000). These widely differing circumstances may lead to a significant gap in performance from the day children enter school for the first time. Consider this data from the *Statistical Abstract of the United States 2010*:

- Only 26% of children ages 3 to 5 from impoverished homes have three or four of the school readiness skills (identified as knowing letters, counting to 20 or higher, writing their name, and reading or pretending to read), compared to 75% of children from families in the middle and higher income ranges.
- Only 48% of children below the poverty threshold can count to 20 or higher, while 67% of those above the threshold can.

Several studies demonstrate the positive impact of early intervention to improve the development and cognition of vulnerable young children from low-income families. These programs typically combine early childhood education with outreach to families that encourages parents to read to their children daily and support their educational endeavors. For example, the High/Scope Perry Preschool Program in Ypsilanti, Michigan, performed a study of early care and education of 3- and 4-year-olds from low-income families. From 1962 to 1967, the early childhood educators worked with these children in preschool during the week. The teachers also went to their homes once a week to help teach the parents what they could do to support their children's cognitive development. When the children in the study turned 40, researchers compared their current lives with those of peers who did not participate in the early education program. The findings showed that half of the preschool children were performing at grade level by age 14, compared to 15% of the control group. Forty-four percent more of the Perry Preschoolers graduated from high school, and 60% were earning upward of $20,000 a year in their 40s, compared to 40% of the control group (Schaefer, Gates, & Kiernan, 2010).

Two other programs from the 1960s and 1970s provided noteworthy results on the power of intensive early childhood education to reduce academic achievement disparities related to socioeconomic status (Tayler, 2013). The Abecedarian Project provided full-day, year-round care for children from low-income households for their first five years, and the Child-Parent Centers emphasized parent involvement and access to health and nutrition services. Long-term monitoring as these children progressed through school and later entered the workforce found higher achievement on standardized tests and graduation rates and lower unemployment, compared to a random control group of children from a similar demographic. These findings "highlight the importance of designing comprehensive cognitive development programs that begin at birth" (Tayler, 2013, p. 25).

Modeling a Love of Learning

Among parents struggling to pay the rent and buy food for their families, taking time to read with their children and engage in learning activities may seem like a luxury they can't afford. Early childhood educators can help to fill that gap by providing an enriched learning environment that supports early literacy and cognitive development. A prime aspect of that environment is your serving as "lead learner" and modeling the joy that can come from learning new things. "A teacher who is passionate and curious is far more likely to generate these characteristics in his or her students from poverty—or for that matter, any student—than someone who is dispassionate about knowledge" (Wilson and Conyers, 2010, p. 207). Furthermore, keep these core concepts and teaching strategies in mind when interacting with children from low-income homes and neighborhoods:

- Students learn in their own way and at their own speed. Options and choices boost motivation.
- Teachers with a wide repertoire of teaching strategies reach more learners more often.
- Providing options and choices reduces the probability of classroom management issues.
- To facilitate the power of options in learning, find ways to work with your colleagues to identify different ways for students to learn the same material. Make full use of cooperative learning settings and have small groups working on a range of different approaches for solving the same problem (Wilson & Conyers, 2010, p. 208).

MAKING LEARNING CONNECTIONS WITH PARENTS

Certainly an ongoing theme of this text has been the importance of having adults in young children's lives who will guide and direct them through their many opportunities for learning and growth. Loving guidance and direction begins at home but continues in settings outside the home such as child-care centers, preschools, and community-based programs. Early childhood educators need to communicate with parents what their goals and expectations are for their children, both in person at parent-teacher conferences and in writing through regular correspondence home (e-mail makes that easy these days). Bringing a child's potential to fruition is a collaborative effort that requires everyone pulling together in the same direction to achieve the desired results.

One concept that we as educators have focused on is bridging—transferring what children learn in an education setting to what is meaningful and important in their own lives. We encourage the use of a bridging component in every lesson, whereby children are encouraged to think about how what they have just learned can be used in other areas of their life, such as in social interactions or in interactions with their parents (Wilson & Conyers, 2011b).

Eliot (1999) stresses the importance of the quality of interactions that parents and other caregivers have with children—that is, making the most of your time together. Even simple interactions, such as a walk to the car or reading a story, can teach important lessons:

> We teach directly when we deliberately show them how something works, explain what we're doing, or reinforce their own explorations with positive attention or negative feedback. And we reach indirectly through the example we are continually setting. Intellectual success depends on much more than "raw intelligence." Smarter children are inevitably more curious about the world, more motivated to explore and ask questions, and more persistent in finding answers, and all these qualities can be shaped to an important degree by parent/caregiver modeling. (Eliot, 1999, p. 451)

Engaging With Educators

Brooke Bugg, who teaches kindergartners at W. C. Britt Elementary School in Snellville, Georgia, says she gets positive responses from parents when she updates them about learning themes and activities in her classroom and shares ideas to keep the learning going at home.

"I've been giving them tips on simple things that are free, activities that they can do at home to help their kids be better students," she says. "When they feel

like they're partners in education with their children, they get excited, and they want to be a part of what their children are doing. . . . They want to do whatever they can to help their children get ahead."

OFFERING ADDITIONAL SUPPORT FOR TEEN PARENTS

In your work in early childhood education, you may encounter teen parents who have limited resources and lack the maturity required to deal well with the challenges facing their children. The phenomenon of "children parenting children" is troubling on several levels, both for the young mothers and their infants. Pregnant teens are less likely to receive adequate prenatal care and more likely to deliver low birth-weight babies. They are less likely to be able to continue their own education and to provide a stimulating environment to support the healthy development of their infants and toddlers.

Despite falling birth rates among 15- to 19-year-olds, teen pregnancy rates in the United States remain higher than in many other developed countries. Teenage births in the United States were estimated to cost taxpayers at least $10.9 billion in 2008. Most of the costs come from the negative consequences for the children of teen mothers, such as increased health care costs, foster care, incarceration, and lost tax revenue (The National Campaign to Prevent Teen and Unplanned Pregnancy, 2011). About 25% of teenage girls who give birth have another baby within 2 years (March of Dimes, 2009).

Researchers continue to investigate what type of social and institutional support will provide the best possible outcomes for teen parents and their children. For example, a research review by the Teen Parent Child Care Quality Improvement Project (2005) found mixed results for teen mothers living at home with their parents; some teenagers reported feeling less stress as a result of the support they received from their family, but others reported negative interactions and more depressive symptoms. Likewise, while some studies reported better health and cognitive development for infants living with their teen mothers and grandmothers, others cautioned that teen parents living at home may be less involved with raising their children. Another study cited reports that early marriage or living with a partner is associated with lower levels of maternal educational achievement and higher school dropout rates. On the other hand, teen parenting programs that involve both parents seem to be more successful in decreasing dropout rates.

One clear conclusion is that teen mothers need support and encouragement to achieve their own educational goals and to provide the type of environment their children need to support their physical and cognitive development.

MAKING THE MOST OF DIVERSITY

Early childhood educators also should take opportunities to embrace the diversity of the children under their supervision. This not only speaks to the various ethnicities and social backgrounds that might be represented in a preschool classroom but also to the possibility that some children might have physical or emotional disabilities as described in this chapter. There are a variety of ways educators can integrate celebration of diversity into a classroom setting, such as the following:

- leading age-appropriate discussions to explore how everyone is similar and how everyone is different;
- reading aloud storybooks that celebrate acceptance of all races, cultures, and abilities (examples include *It's Okay to Be Different* by Todd Parr and *Special People, Special Ways* by Arlene Maguire);
- providing dolls and play set figures in the toy area that depict different races and skin tones;
- teaching children to count or say the alphabet in other languages besides English;
- teaching basic words in American Sign Language, such as "please" and "thank you"; and
- displaying photos and posters that depict our multiracial, multicultural world.

Learning how to accept and celebrate diversity at an early age is something that will stay with children for a lifetime. One of greatest challenges for children with disabilities and/or socioeconomic disadvantages is dealing with the negative connotations of "being different," which shuts them out of interactions with their peers and exacerbates the adversities they already face. By teaching children to reach out in friendship to a diverse range of their peers, early childhood educators and other caring adults provide a gift of meaningful personal relationships built on seeing people for who they really are rather than dismissing them with a label. This enriches the lives of all children who open themselves up to the experience of learning from adults and learning from each other, providing them with the opportunity to flourish from young childhood well into adulthood.

☆PRACTICAL TIPS FOR EARLY CHILDHOOD EDUCATORS☆

Addressing and Mitigating Risks to Healthy Child Development

Recognize that every child is unique. Tailor your interactions to identify and teach to each child's learning needs and strengths. Emphasize the uniqueness of each child. Remember that each child's brain is shaped by a combination of genetic and environmental factors, resulting in an individual blend of strengths and areas where he or she might benefit from intensive support for learning. Spend time regularly with individual children to get to know them and their interests and to develop a caring relationship.

Involve parents in their children's cognitive development—in your program and at home. This can be achieved through a variety of opportunities. Hold regular parent meetings to keep them informed. Send e-mails, text messages, tweets, and correspondence home to update parents on their children's progress and share learning activities they can do at home. Prepare a regular class newsletter. Get to know the parents by offering volunteer opportunities for field trips and scheduling regular visits to the classroom. Collaborate with community organizations that have family programs, and encourage full participation of parents and siblings to get to know the support network for the children whom you are teaching.

Connect with other educational, health, and child development professionals. This is especially useful for children with learning disabilities or challenges because it helps facilitate connections to support child development and healthy families. In author Donna Wilson's work as a school psychologist, she found that many professionals in the community—physicians, child psychologists, public librarians, and recreation directors, for example—are willing to volunteer their time to address the needs of children and to help forge school-community partnerships in support of education.

Acknowledge and celebrate diversity. Learning to communicate and interact with people from different backgrounds will be an increasingly important skill for young children as they enter school and later go on to college and the working world. The earlier you start helping children understand and embrace diversity, the more effective and long-lasting your efforts will be.

NOTE

This chapter is adapted, updated, and expanded with permission from "Ten Risk Factors," Chapter 2 of *BrainSMART Early Start: Building the Brain Power of Young Children* (2nd ed.), by Donna Wilson, Lola Heverly, and Marcus Conyers (BrainSMART, 2011).

Conclusion

With all the astonishing discoveries about how young children learn and advances in applying that research, this is an exciting time for the field of early childhood development. Let's recap some of those key findings and implications for how early childhood educators, parents, and other caregivers can guide infants, toddlers, and preschoolers to make the most of their learning potential.

Babies are born with their brains fully ready to learn. They are fascinated by the sights, sounds, smells, tastes, and touch of the world around them and are especially engaged by the faces, voices, and embraces of loved ones. Their imitations of facial movements, sounds, and gestures are not just instinctive, but a powerful means of learning by doing.

Experience shapes intellect. Contrary to persistent assumptions that pervade American culture, intelligence is not fixed from birth. Genetics do play a role in establishing an intelligence baseline, but experience also has a strong influence on intellectual development. In short, learning can make us functionally smarter—and *all* children can learn. Research on brain plasticity supports the view of intellectual, cognitive, and emotional development as malleable and changeable throughout life. No longer should children have to endure such lifelong labels as "bad at math," "struggling reader," "klutzy," or even "painfully shy." These deficits are not permanent attributes. Through persistent effort, deliberate practice, and effective instructional support, the vast majority of children can improve their cognitive, social, motor, and self-regulatory skills. This new understanding of malleable intelligence has crucial implications for the learning potential of children, adolescents, teenagers, and adults—even for parents and teachers as lifelong learners!

The brain and body work together to support learning. Nutritious eating habits, regular physical activity, and adequate sleep not only support healthy physical development but also keep the brain in peak learning condition. Thus, it is essential to start young children off right with healthy habits.

Emotions also influence how well young children learn. The optimal learning environment exudes positivity and makes children feel safe, secure, valued, and encouraged to take intellectual risks without fear of ridicule for being "wrong." Young children can be taught an optimistic, can-do approach to learning, and this belief that they can and will succeed will serve them well throughout life.

Learning to wield cognitive skills supports school readiness. Toddlers and preschoolers can begin to learn thinking strategies that will support development of literacy, problem-solving, critical-thinking, and communication skills. This idea of "learning how to learn" may be new to many parents and even early childhood educators who grew up thinking about education as the pursuit of knowledge on how to read, write, and do math and science. However, preparing children to flourish in the 21st century requires helping them develop a wider skill set of cognitive (thinking and reasoning), intrapersonal (regulating one's behaviors and emotions to achieve goals), and interpersonal (relating to others and understanding others' points of view) competencies (Pellegrino & Hilton, 2012). Throughout this text, we introduced examples of teaching young children to begin developing these competencies, such as focusing their attention on important tasks, learning to listen better, and comparing and classifying.

Learning self-control is an important precursor to success in school and in life. We use the metaphor of teaching children to be "the boss of their brain." Children are better able to take in information if they pay attention, resist distractions, have a clear intent about what they want to achieve, and persist in the often hard work required to accomplish their goals. We can begin to equip young children with the competency of self-control through stories and examples about the benefits of self-regulation, modeling, hints and reminders, and explicit praise for taking charge of their behavior.

Young children need unconditional affection but benefit from conditional praise. In other words, every child should be loved and appreciated for being his or her own unique self. Educational researchers and psychologists tend to agree that praise is most effective in support of learning when it emphasizes effort and accomplishment in proportion with the achievement. Engaging with young children about their hard work, ideas, and processes motivates them to persist until they master new skills and accomplish their goals.

It is never too late to address risks to healthy child development. Toxic stress stemming from poverty, food insecurity, unstable home environments, or unsafe neighborhoods may impair young children's development—but not their potential to learn and catch up when their basic needs are provided for and they receive intensive instructional support. Early childhood educators must work with parents, other caregivers, and educational and community leaders to improve supports for families and connect them with helpful resources. The families of children with developmental and learning disabilities also benefit from connections to medical, social services, and educational professionals and programs. Environmental inequities pose significant challenges, but working together, we can do our best to ensure that all children can flourish in their early years—and beyond.

Acknowledgments

In applying the practical implications of mind, brain, and education research to early childhood development, we have had many inspiring conversations with and input from colleagues and friends teaching and conducting research at universities, as well as those teaching in school-based and community preschool programs. We look forward to continuing our discussions with fellow members of the American Educational Research Association (AERA), including Debby Zambo at Brain, Neurosciences, and Education Special Interest Group meetings; AERA Division K (Teaching and Teacher Education) member Susan M. Benner; and teacher educator Marcia Stewart.

We would also like to thank Lola Heverly, who worked with Marcus on a statewide initiative for early childhood educators in Florida, and Sarah Sprinkel, who has worked tirelessly for young children at the district level in Orlando, in the community of Winter Park, and at the state level in Florida. And we thank these administrators and teachers who have graciously permitted us to share stories from their schools and classrooms and their perspectives on early childhood education: Karen Sinclair and Cari Rotenberger, respectively director and assistant director of the First Congregational Church Weekday Preschool and Kindergarten, Winter Park, Florida; Brooke Bugg, kindergarten teacher, W. C. Britt Elementary School, Snellville, Georgia; Regina Cabadaidis, preschool/kindergarten teacher, S. D. Spady Elementary School, Delray Beach, Florida; Diane Hickey, preschool teacher, Washington Elementary School, Union, New Jersey; and Christena Nelson, kindergarten teacher, Copper Canyon Elementary School, West Jordan, Utah. These teachers and administrators earned their graduate degrees with a major in brain-based teaching in programs we codeveloped at Nova Southeastern University's Abraham S. Fischler School of Education. Their stories of teaching and learning with young children always inspire us!

We have greatly enjoyed working with Nancy Evans, our acquisitions editor with Rowman & Littlefield. Finally, our thanks to our editing team, Karen Bankston and Diane Franklin, for their skill, precision, and patience as we continued to add new research and concepts to successive versions of this text.

Donna Wilson and Marcus Conyers

Glossary

AEIOU learning cycle Representation of the learning cycle in five stages: attention, exploration, inquiry, order, and understanding and use; this cycle occurs as the human brain becomes aware of new knowledge, processes the concepts and information, and then applies the new knowledge and skills.

Attention The ability to focus on a specific object, task, or piece of information without being distracted by extraneous stimuli. There are two forms of attention: *bottom-up*, which is activated by the stimuli around you, and *top-down*, which is the deliberate focus of your brain on a specific task.

Attention cycle The periods in which the brain shifts in and out of high attention. The highest levels of attention in this cycle are typically at the beginning and end, referred to as *primacy* and *recency*.

Attention deficit hyperactivity disorder (ADHD) A neurobehavioral disorder characterized by pervasive inattention, hyperactivity, and impulsivity.

Autism A neural development disorder characterized by impairment in communication and in developing social relationships. The term *autism spectrum disorders (ASD)* encompasses a range of disorders with such characteristics.

Axon Long, unbranched fiber on a neuron that carries nerve impulses away from the cell to the next cell; see also *neuron, dendrite,* and *synapse.*

Body-Brain System Refers to the way that the body and brain work together to accomplish learning.

Bottom-up attention system See *attention.*

Brain hemispheres Right and left sides of the brain.

Brain plasticity The brain's capability to adapt to changes and new information by forming new neural connections throughout life; also known as *neuroplasticity*.

Brainstem One of the three major parts of the brain; it receives sensory input and monitors vital functions such as the heartbeat, body temperature, and digestion.

Broca's area An area in the brain's frontal lobe that is associated with the production of speech and other linguistic functions.

Central nervous system The part of the body that encompasses the brain and spinal cord.

Cerebellum Cauliflower-shaped structure below the brain's occipital lobe; current research suggests that this part of the brain coordinates muscle movement and is linked to cognition, novelty, and emotions.

Cerebral cortex See *neocortex*.

Cerebrum The largest of the three major parts of the brain; it is composed of the left and right hemispheres and controls sensory interpretation, thinking, and memory.

Chromosome disorders Disorders characterized by an abnormal number of chromosomes, either more or fewer than the typical 46; an example is Down syndrome, wherein children are born with an extra copy of chromosome 21.

Clear intent The task of identifying a goal and how to achieve it.

Code-related skills The ability to decode and encode text as required for reading and writing.

Cognitive assets Thinking strategies you can teach and young children can learn and incorporate into their play, problem solving, and interaction with others.

Cognitive development Construction of thought processes, including perception, problem solving, decision making, and memory.

Corpus callosum Bridge of nerve fibers connecting the left and right cerebral hemispheres and facilitating communication between them.

Cortisol Steroid hormone that is released as the brain responds to stressful situations.

Critical period See *sensitive period.*

Critical thinking Ability to think analytically or reflectively to determine a course of action or to formulate a set of beliefs.

Dendrite Branched extension from the cell body of a neuron that receives impulses from nearby neurons through synaptic contacts; see also *neuron, axon,* and *synapse.*

DNA Deoxyribonucleic acid, the main component of living tissue that contains the genetic code responsible for inheritance and transmission of chromosomes and genes.

Down syndrome A chromosomal disorder caused by the presence of an extra copy of chromosome 21.

Emerging literacy Period during which a child is developing the abilities required to read and write.

Executive function Set of cognitive processes that occur in the brain to organize thoughts and activities, set priorities, manage time, and accomplish goals; related to *self-control* and *working memory.*

Experience-dependent synaptogenesis See *synaptogenesis.*

Experience-expectant plasticity See *synaptogenesis*.

Explicit memories See *memory*.

Exuberant synaptogenesis Periods of rapid development, for example, during infancy; this period usually peaks around 10 months of age; see also *synaptogenesis*.

Fetal alcohol syndrome Pattern of congenital abnormalities in a child caused by consumption of alcohol by the pregnant mother. The term *fetal alcohol spectrum disorders (FASD)* describes a range of disorders that may encompass a variety of physical, mental, and emotional impairments.

Flourish To grow luxuriantly, to achieve success.

Focus Ability to remain alert and fix one's attention on a specific point, purpose, or task.

Food insecurity Limited availability or uncertainty about the availability of nutritional foods.

Frontal lobe One of four main areas of each hemisphere of the cerebrum; this lobe controls voluntary movement, verbal expression, problem solving, willpower, and planning.

Glial cells Special "glue" cells in the brain that surround each neuron, providing support, protection, and nourishment.

Habituation Characterized by monotony—giving the brain too much of one signal, such as one sound (monotone) or one voice (monologue)—thus causing a child to tune out and be more prone to distractions; also known as *neuronal habituation*.

Hippocampus Part of the brain involved in short-term to long-term memory processing.

Implicit memories See *memory*.

Limbic system Structures at the base of the cerebrum that control emotions; the five major structures are the thalamus, hypothalamus, basal ganglia, amygdala, and hippocampus.

Locomotor skills Ability to move from place to place.

Low birth weight Defined as an infant who weighs less than 2,500 grams (approximately 5½ pounds) at birth.

Malleable intelligence Principle that intelligence is not a fixed trait but rather can be enhanced through experiences and environmental influences; see also *brain plasticity*.

Memory Process by which the brain stores and retrieves information; *explicit* memories are those tied to specific experiences, whereas *implicit* memories are skills and knowledge the brain retains without recalling the experience of learning them.

Metacognition Act of thinking about one's thinking with the aim of identifying strategies useful for solving a problem at hand and improving one's use of those strategies.

Mirror neurons Special cells in the brain that are activated when seeing someone perform an action and that cause the individual's brain to respond as if his or her body were doing the same action.

Mnemonic Memory device that reduces a large body of information to a shorter, more memorable form by using a letter to represent each shortened piece of information.

Modeling Demonstrating appropriate behavior and social skills with the objective of having others learn and exhibit similar behavior and skills themselves.

Monogenetic disorders Disorders caused by mutation in a single gene.

Motherese Exaggerated and repetitive speech patterns that many adults naturally adopt when talking with babies.

Motor cortex Part of the brain that receives and uses information to carry out body movements.

Myelin White, fatty substance that forms in segments to surround and insulate a neuron's axon; myelin is responsible for the color of the white matter in the brain and spinal cord.

Myelination Process of surrounding and insulating neurons to facilitate faster transmission of nerve impulses.

Neocortex The outer folded layer of the brain that covers the cerebrum and cerebellum; plays an important role in memory and higher-order information processing; also known as *cerebral cortex*.

Neuron Basic cell of the nervous system, consisting of a long fiber called an axon, which transmits impulses, and many shorter fibers, called dendrites, which receive them; the three main types of neurons are sensory, association, and motor; see also *axon, dendrite,* and *synapse.*

Neuronal habituation See *habituation.*

Neuroplasticity See *brain plasticity.*

Nonimmediate talk Conversations with children that extend reading experiences.

Occipital lobe One of four areas of the brain; primarily involved in the ability to see and perceive visual information.

Parietal lobe One of four areas in the brain; deals with the reception of sensory input and plays a role in reading, writing, language, and calculation.

Phoneme Smallest unit of speech, as in the k-sound in *cat,* that distinguishes one word or utterance from another.

Phonemic awareness Ability to hear and identify the smallest structural units of sound in a language; see also *phoneme*.

Plasticity See *brain plasticity*.

Positive stress See *toxic stress*.

Postural skills Ability to position the body.

Practical optimism Strategy for learning that fosters positive expectations as a means of optimizing positive outcomes.

Prefrontal cortex Part of the brain associated with the ability to regulate and express emotion and to think and plan.

Preterm birth Birth that occurs at less than 37 weeks of gestation.

Primacy See *attention cycle*.

Prosody Rhythm and speech intonations of spoken language.

Pruning Process through which neural connections created as a result of experiences that are not repeated are eliminated.

Pygmalion effect Influence that expectations can have on student achievement.

Receny See *attention cycle*.

Scaffolding Learning process that builds on skills children already possess and provides support to help them develop additional skills and achieve subsequent learning goals via guidance from an adult or more knowledgeable peer.

Self-control Ability to control detrimental behavior, emotions, and impulses and/or to stay focused on a required task without giving in to distractions; considered part of *executive function*; also known as *self-regulation*.

Self-regulation See *self-control*.

Sensitive period Time when a particular part of the brain is most apt to change and most vulnerable to environmental influences; also known as *critical period*.

Social play Most sophisticated form of play; often involves pretending and role-playing.

Synapse Microscopic gap between the axon of one neuron and the dendrite of the next neuron where the neurotransmitters are released to stimulate the next neuron; it is the junction communication point where neurons interact; see also *neuron, axon,* and *dendrite*.

Synaptogenesis Process through which the brain creates new synapses. There are two types: *experience expectant,* which refers to experiences that are common to all humans and important for typical development, such as learning to walk and talk; and *experience dependent,* which happens in response to experiences with people, places, and things. See also *exuberant synaptogenesis*.

Temporal lobe One of four areas of the brain primarily invovled in the organization of sensory input, auditory perception, speech and language production, and memoy formation.

Theory of mind Ability to predict or surmise how others might think and react in a certain situation based on one's own personal experience.

Tolerable stress See *toxic stress*.

Top-down attention system See *attention*.

Toxic stress Harmful form of stress characterized by strong, frequent, or prolonged activation of the body's stress management system due to chronic, uncontrollable stress events in the child's life that are often endured without the support of a caring adult. Other forms of stress include *positive stress,* which is part of normal, everyday life, and *tolerable stress,* which occurs as part of a traumatic event in the child's life but is made manageable by the presence of a caring adult.

Transfer Influence of past learning on new learning and the degree to which new learning will be useful to the learner's future.

Vestibular system Sensory system that controls the sense of movement and balance.

Wernicke's area Area in the brain's frontal lobe that has been identified as being integral to language comprehension.

Working memory Temporary memory where information is processed consciously and used to solve immediate problems; part of *executive function*.

References

Aamodt, S., & Wang, S. (2011). *Welcome to your child's brain*. New York, NY: Bloomsbury.

Achor, S. (2010). *The happiness advantage: The seven principles of positive psychology that fuel success and performance at work*. New York, NY: Crown Business.

American Academy of Sleep Medicine. (2009, June 15). Better sleep is associated with improved academic success. *ScienceDaily*. Retrieved from http://www.sciencedaily.com/releases/2009/06/090610091232.htm

Anda, R. F., Felitti, V. J., Bremner, J. D., Walker, J. D., Whitfield, C., Perry, B. D., Dube, S. R., & Giles, W. H. (2006). The enduring effects of abuse and related adverse experiences in childhood. *European Archives of Psychiatry and Clinical Neuroscience, 256*(3), 174–186.

Autism Society. (n.d.). Causes. Retrieved from http://www.autism-society.org/about-autism/causes

Aylward, G. P. (1997). *Infant and early childhood neuropsychology*. New York, NY: Plenum Press.

Bandura, A. (1977). *Social learning theory*. Englewood Cliffs, NJ: Prentice Hall.

Barnet, A. B., & Barnet, R. J. (1998). *The youngest minds: Parenting and genes in the development of intellect and emotion*. New York, NY: Simon & Shuster.

Begley, S. (1997, February 28). How to build a baby's brain. *Newsweek*. Retrieved from http://www.newsweek.com/1997/02/28/how-to-build-a-baby-s-brain.html

Berk, L. E. (2001). *Awakening children's minds: How parents and teachers can make a difference*. New York, NY: Oxford University Press.

Berninger, V. W., & Richards, T. L. (2002). *Brain literacy for educators and psychologists*. San Diego, CA: Academic Press.

Blair, C. (2003). Self-regulation and school readiness. *Eric Digest*. Retrieved from http://ecap.crc.illinois.edu/eecearchive/digests/2003/blair03.pdf

Blair, C., & Diamond, A. (2008). Biological processes in prevention and intervention: The promotion of self-regulation as a means of preventing school failure. *Development and Psychopathology, 20*, 899–911. doi:10.1017/S0954579408000436.

Blakeslee, S. (2006, January 10). Mirror neurons: Cells that read minds. *The New York Times*. Retrieved from http://nytimes.com/2006/01/10/science/10mirr.html?_r=1pagewanted=all

Bono, G., & Froh, J. (2009). Gratitude in school: Benefits to students and schools. In R. Gilman, E. S. Huebner, & M. J. Furlong (Eds.), *Handbook of positive psychology in schools* (pp. 77–88). New York, NY: Routledge.

Bransford, J., Brown, A., & Cocking, R. (Eds.). (2000). *How people learn: Brain, mind, experience, and school* (Expanded ed.). Washington, DC: National Academy Press.

Bronson, P., & Merryman, A. (2009). *NurtureShock: New thinking about children*. New York, NY: Twelve.

153

Brooks, D. (2011). *The social animal: The hidden sources of love, character, and achievement.* New York, NY: Random House.

Bruer, J. T. (1999). *The myth of the first three years.* New York, NY: The Free Press.

Bruner, J. S. (1966). *Toward a theory of instruction.* Cambridge, MA: Harvard University Press.

Buss, C., Entringer, S., Swanson, J. M., & Wadhwa, P. (2012). The role of stress in brain development: The gestational environment's long-term effects on the brain. *Cerebrum, 4.* Retrieved from http://www.ncbi.nlm.nih.gov/pmc/articles/PMC3574809

Caine, R. N., Caine, G., Klimek, K. J., & McClintic, C. L. (2008). *Twelve brain/mind learning principles in action: Developing executive function of the human brain* (2nd ed.). Thousand Oaks, CA: Sage.

Cambourne, B. (2001a). Conditions for literacy learning: Why do some students fail to learn to read? Ockham's razor and the conditions of learning. *The Reading Teacher, (54)8,* 784–786.

Cambourne, B. (2001b). Conditions for literacy learning: Turning learning theory into classroom instruction. A minicase study. *The Reading Teacher, 54*(4), 414–429.

Carlson, S. M., Moses, L. J., & Breton, C. (2002). How specific is the relation between executive function and theory of mind? Contributions of inhibitory control and working memory. *Infant and Child Development, 11,* 73–92. doi:10.1002/icd.298. Retrieved from http://pavlov.psyc.vuw.ac.nz/courses/Psyc%20443/415%20Papers/Carlson_et_at.pdf

The Center for Accelerated Learning. (n.d.). What is accelerated learning? Retrieved from http://www.alcenter.com/what_is.php

Centers for Disease Control and Prevention. (2009). Tobacco use and pregnancy. Retrieved from http://www.cdc.gov/reproductivehealth/tobaccousepregnancy/index.htm

Centers for Disease Control and Prevention. (2010). Increasing prevalence of parent-reported attention-deficit/hyperactivity disorder among children—United States, 2003 and 2007. *Morbidity and mortality weekly report, 49*(44), 1439–1443. Retrieved from http://www.cdc.gov/mmwr/preview/mmwrhtml/mm5944a3.htm?s_cid=mm5944a3_w

Centers for Disease Control and Prevention. (2012a, March 12). CDC estimates 1 in 88 children in United States has been identified as having an autism spectrum disorder [Press release]. Retrieved from http://www.cdc.gov/media/releases/2012/p0329_autism_disorder.html

Centers for Disease Control and Prevention. (2012b). *Key findings: Alcohol use and binge drinking among women of childbearing age—United States, 2006–2010.* Retrieved from http://www.cdc.gov/ncbddd/fasd/kf-alcohol-use2006-2010.html

Centre for Educational Research and Innovation (Eds). (2007). *Understanding the brain: The birth of a learning science.* Danvers, MA: Organisation for Economic Co-operation and Development.

Child Trends Data Bank. (2012). *Late or no prenatal care: Indicators on children and youth.* Retrieved from http://www.childtrendsdatabank.org/sites/default/files/25_Prenatal_Care.pdf

Children's Defense Fund. (2010). *The state of America's children 2010 report.* Retrieved from http://www.childrensdefense.org/child-research-data-publications/data/state-of-americas-children.pdf

Chugani, H. T., & Phelps, M. E. (1991). Imaging human brain development with positron emission tomography. *The Journal of Nuclear Medicine, 32*(1), 23–26.

Coleman-Jensen, A., Nord, M., Andres, M., & Carlson, S. (2012). Household food security in the United States in 2011. *U.S. Department of Agriculture, Economic Research Service, Economic Research Report, 141.* Retrieved from http://www.ers.usda.gov/media/884525/err141.pdf

Conkling, W. (2001). *Smart-wiring your baby's brain.* New York, NY: HarperCollins.

Conyers, M. A., & Wilson, D. L. (2009). *Introduction to BrainSMART HealthWise* (2nd ed.). Orlando, FL: BrainSMART.

Crain-Thoreson, C., & Dale, P. S. (1992). Do early talkers become early readers? Linguistic precocity, preschool language, and emergent literacy. *Developmental Psychology, 28*(3), 421–429.

Cunningham, A. E., & Stanovich, K. E. (1998). What reading does for the mind. *American Educator, 22*(1-2), 8–15. Retrieved from http://www.keithstanovich.com/Site/Research_on_Reading_files/Cunningham_Stano_Amer_Educator_1998.pdf

Daro, D. (2010). *Child abuse prevention: A job half done.* Chicago: Chapin Hall at the University of Chicago. Retrieved from http://www.chapinhall.org/sites/default/files/publications/Child%20Abuse_IB_F_02_25_10.pdf

Davidson, R. J., with Begley, S. (2012). *The emotional life of your brain.* New York, NY: Hudson Street Press.

DeTemple, J. M. (2001). Parents and children reading books together. In D. K. Dickinson & P. O. Tabors (Eds.), *Young children learning at home and school: Beginning literacy with language* (pp. 31–52). Baltimore, MD: Brookes.

Dickinson, D. K. (2001a). Book reading in preschool classrooms: Is recommended practice common? In D. K. Dickinson & P. O. Tabors (Eds.), *Young children learning at home and school: Beginning literacy with language* (pp. 175–204). Baltimore, MD: Brookes.

Dickinson, D. K. (2001b). Large-group and free-play times: Conversational settings supporting language and literacy development. In D. K. Dickinson & P. O. Tabors (Eds.), *Young children learning at home and school: Beginning literacy with language* (pp. 223–256). Baltimore, MD: Brookes.

Dickinson, D. K., & Tabors, P. O. (2002). Fostering language and literacy in classrooms and homes. *Young Children, 57*(2), 10–18. Retrieved from http://faculty.tamu-commerce.edu/jthompson/Resources/DickinsonTaborFosteringlanguageLiteracy.pdf

Draganski, B., Gaser, C., Kempermann, G., Kuhn, H. G., Winkler, J., Buchel, C., & May, A. (2006). Temporal and spatial dynamics of brain structure changes during extensive learning. *The Journal of Neuroscience, 26*(23), 6314–6317.

Duckworth, A.L., & Seligman, M. E. P. (2005). Self-discipline outdoes IQ in predicting academic performance of adolescents. *Psychological Science, 16*(12), 939–944. Retrieved from http://www.sas.upenn.edu/~duckwort/images/PsychologicalScience Dec2005.pdf

Dweck, C. S. (2006). *Mindset, the new psychology of success: How we can learn to fulfill our potential.* New York, NY: Bantam Books.

Dweck, C. S., Mangels, J. A., & Good C. (2004). Motivational effects of attention, cognition, and performance. In D. Y. Dai & R. J. Sternberg (Eds.), *Motivation, emotion, and cognition: Integrated perspectives on intellectual functioning* (pp. 41–55). Mahwah, NJ: Erlbraum.

Eliot, L. (1999). *What's going on in there? How the brain and mind develop in the first five years of life.* New York, NY: Bantam Books.

Faraone, S. V., Perlis, R. H., Doyle, A. E., Smoller, J. W., Goralnick, J. J., Holmgren, M. A., & Sklar, P. (2005). Molecular genetics of attention-deficit/hyperactivity disorder. *Biological Psychiatry, 57*(11), 1313–1323.

Feerick, M. M., & Silverman, G. B. (Eds.). (2006). *Children exposed to violence*. Baltimore, MD: Brookes.

Fenson, L., Marchman, V. A., Thal, D. J., Dale, P. S., Reznick, J. S., & Bates, E. (2007). *MacArthur-Bates communicative development inventories: User's guide and technical manual* (2nd ed.). Baltimore, MD: Brookes.

Fernald, A. (1985). Four-month-old infants prefer to listen to motherese. *Infant Behavior and Development, 8*, 181–195. Retrieved from http://psych.stanford.edu/~babylab/pdfs/Fernald%201985.pdf

Florez, I. R. (2011). Developing young children's self-regulation through everyday experiences. *Young Children, 66*(4), 46–51. Retrieved from http://www.naeyc.org/files/yc/file/201107/Self-Regulation_Florez_OnlineJuly2011.pdf

Frank, M. G., Issa, N. P., & Stryker, M. P. (2001). Sleep enhances plasticity in the developing visual cortex. *Neuron, 30*, 275–287. Retrieved from http://www.cscb.northwestern.edu/jcpdfs/frank01.pdf

Frederickson, B. (2009). *Positivity*. New York, NY: Crown.

Frost, N. L. (1998). *Neuroscience, play, and child development*. Paper presented at the IPA/USA Triennial National Conference, Longmont, CO. ERIC Document 427845, PS 027 328. Retrieved from http://www.eric.ed.gov

Galinsky, E. (2010). *Mind in the making*. New York, NY: HarperCollins.

Gallotta, M. C., Guidetti, L., Franciosi, E., Emerenziani, G. P., Bonavolonta, V., & Baldari, C. (2012). Effects of varying type of exertion on children's attention capacity. *Medicine & Science in Sports & Exercise, 44*(3), 550–555. doi:10.1249/MSS.0b013e3182305552

Gardner, H. (2006). *Multiple intelligences: New horizons in theory and practice* (Rev. ed.). New York, NY: Basic Books.

Gazzaniga, M. (1989). Organization of the human brain. *Science, 245*(4921), 947–952. doi:10.1126/science.2672334

Geoffroy, M-C., Coté, S. M., Parent, S., Seguin, J. R. (2006). Daycare attendance, stress, and mental health. *The Canadian Journal of Psychiatry, 51*, 607–615. Retrieved from http://ww1.cpa-apc.org:8080/publications/archives/cjp/2006/august/geoffroy-rp.asp

Gibb, B. J. (2007). *The rough guide to the brain*. New York, NY: Penguin Putnam.

Giedd, J. (n.d.) Inside the teenage brain: Interview Jay Giedd. *PBS Frontline*. Retrieved from http://www.pbs.org/wgbh/pages/frontline/shows/teenbrain/interviews/giedd.html

Gilman, R., Huebner, E. S., & Furlong, M. J. (2009). *Handbook of positive psychology in schools*. New York, NY: Routledge.

Goldberg, E. (2009). *The new executive brain: Frontal lobes in a complex world*. New York, NY: Oxford University Press.

Goodman, J. C., Dale, P. S., & Li, P. (2008). Does frequency count? Parental input and the acquisition of vocabulary. *Journal of Child Language, 35*(3), 515–531.

Goswami, U. (2008). *Cognitive development: The learning brain*. New York, NY: Psychology Press.

Greenough, W. T., & Black, J. E. (1992). Induction of brain structure by experience: Substrates for cognitive development. In M. Gunnar & C. Nelson (Eds.), *Developmental behavior neuroscience* (Vol. 24, pp. 155–200). Hillsdale, NJ: Erlbaum.

Gregory, G. H., & Parry, T. (2006). *Designing brain-compatible learning* (3rd ed.). Thousand Oaks, CA: Corwin Press.

Guralnick, M. J. (1998). Effectiveness of early intervention for vulnerable children: A developmental perspective. *American Journal on Mental Retardation, 102*(4), 319–345. Retrieved from https://depts.washington.edu/chdd/guralnick/pdfs/effect_EI_AJMR _vol102_98.pdf

Guralnick, M. J. (2005). Early intervention for children with intellectual disabilities. *Journal of Applied Research in Intellectual Disabilities, 18,* 313–324. Retrieved from http://depts.washington.edu/chdd/guralnick/pdfs/ei_jar_18_05.pdf

Guralnick, M. J. (2012). Preventive interventions for preterm children: Effectiveness and developmental mechanisms. *Journal of Development and Behavioral Pediatrics, 33,* 352–364. Retrieved from http://depts.washington.edu/chdd/guralnick/pdfs/ Preventive_Interventions_Preterm_Children.pdf

Hamilton, B. E., Martin, J. A., & Ventura, S. J. (2012). Births: Preliminary data for 2011. *National Vital Statistics Reports, 61*(5). Retrieved from http://www.cdc.gov/nchs/ data/nvsr/nvsr61/nvsr61_05.pdf

Hannaford, C. (2005). *Smart moves: Why learning is not all in your head* (2nd ed.). Salt Lake City, UT: Great River Books.

Hardiman, M. M., & Denckla, M. B. (2010). The science of education: Informing teaching and learning through the brain sciences. In *Cerebrum 2010: Emerging ideas in brain science* (pp. 3–11). Washington, DC: Dana Press.

Harmon, K. (2010, April 30). How important is physical contact with your infant? *Scientific American.* Retrieved from http://www.scientificamerican.com/article.cfm? id=infant-touch

Hart, B., & Risley, T. R. (2003). The early catastrophe: The 30-million-word gap. *American Educator, 27*(1), 4–9.

Hattie, J. A. C. (2009). *Visible learning: A synthesis of over 800 meta-analyses relating to achievement.* New York, NY: Routledge.

Hawley, T. (2000). *Starting smart: How early experiences affect brain development.* Chicago, IL: Ounce of Prevention Fund; Washington, DC: Zero to Three. Retrieved from http://www.ounceofprevention.org/news/pdfs/Starting_Smart.pdf

Hebb, D. O. (1949). *The organization of behavior: A neuropsychological theory.* New York, NY: Wiley.

Hinton, C., Fischer, K. W., & Glennon, C. (2012, March). Students at the center: Mind, brain, and education [Executive Summary]. Retrieved from http://students atthecenter.org/sites/scl.dl-dev.com/files/field_attach_file/Exec_Hinton%26 Fischer%26Glennon_032312.pdf

Hirsh-Pasek, K., Golinkoff, R. M., Berk, L. E., & Singer, D. G. (2009). *A mandate for playful learning: Presenting the evidence.* New York, NY: Oxford University Press.

Howard, P. J. (1999). *The owner's manual for the brain: Applications from mind-brain research.* Austin TX: Bard Press.

Huttenlocher, P. R. (2002). *Neural plasticity: The effects of environment on the development of the cerebral cortex.* Cambridge, MA: Harvard University Press.

Idaho Public Television. (2003). Dialogue for kids: Skin facts. Retrieved from http:// idahoptv.org/dialogue4kids/season5/skin/facts.cfm

Iacoboni, M. (2009). *Mirroring people: The science of empathy and how we connect with others.* New York, NY: Picador.

Immordino-Yang, M. H., & Fischer, K. W. (2007). Dynamic development of hemispheric biases in three cases. In D. Coch, G. Dawson, & K. W. Fischer (Eds.), *Human behavior, learning, and the developing brain* (pp. 74–111). New York, NY: Guilford Press.

James, W. (1890). *The principles of psychology.* New York, NY: Henry Holt.

Johnson, J. A. (2009). *Babies in the rain: Promoting play, exploration, and discovery with infants and toddlers.* St. Paul, MN: Redleaf Press.

Johnston, P. H. (2012). *Opening minds.* Portland, ME: Stenhouse.

Katz, L. G. (1996). Child development knowledge and teacher preparation: Confronting assumptions. *Early Childhood Research Quarterly, 11,* 135–146.

Katz, J. R. (2001). Playing at home: The talk of pretend play. In D. K. Dickinson & P. O. Tabors (Eds.), *Young children learning at home and school: Beginning literacy with language* (pp. 53–74). Baltimore, MD: Brookes.

Keen, R. (2011). The development of problem solving in young children: A critical cognitive skill. *Annual Review of Psychology, 62,* 1–21. doi:10.1146/annurev.psych.031809.130730

Kuhl, P., & Rivera-Gaxiola, M. (2008). Neural substrates of language acquisition. *Annual Review of NeuroScience, 31,* 511–534. Retrieved from http://ilabs.washington.edu/kuhl/pdf/2008_Kuhl_Rivera-Gaxiola.pdf

Kuhn, D. (2000). Metacognitive development. *Current Directions in Psychological Science, 9*(5), 178–181. Retrieved from http://www.mx1.educationforthinking.org/sites/default/files/page-image/1-02MetacognitiveDevelopment.pdf

Lai, E. R. (2011, April). *Metacognition: A literature review.* Pearson's Research Reports. Retrieved from http://www.pearsonassessments.com/hai/images/tmrs/Metacognition_Literature_Review_Final.pdf

Lightfoot, C., Cole, M., & Cole, S. R. (2008). *The development of children* (6th ed.). New York, NY: Worth.

MacLean, P. D. (1990). *The triune brain in evolution.* New York, NY: Plenum Press.

March of Dimes. (2009). Medical resources: Teenage pregnancy. Retrieved from http://www.marchofdimes.com/medicalresources_teenpregnancy.html

March of Dimes. (2010, April). Smoking during pregnancy. Retrieved from http://www.marchofdimes.com/pregnancy/alcohol_smoking.html

Marzano, R. J. (2007). *The art and science of teaching: A comprehensive framework for effective instruction.* Alexandria, VA: Association for Supervision and Curriculum Development.

Medina, J. (2008). *Brain rules: 12 principles for surviving and thriving at work, home, and school.* Seattle, WA: Pear Press.

Medina, J. (2010). *Brain rules for baby: How to raise a smart and happy child from zero to five.* Seattle, WA: Pear Press.

Meltzoff, A. N. (2005). Imitation and other minds: The "like me" hypothesis. In S. Hurley & N. Chater (Eds.), *Perspectives on imitation: From neuroscience to social science* (Vol. 2, pp. 55–77). Cambridge, MA: MIT Press. Retrieved from http://mirrorneurons.free.fr/Meltzoff_Like%20Me%20Hypothesis.pdf

Meltzoff, A. N., Kuhl, P. K., Movellan, J., & Sejnowski, T. J. (2009, July 17). Foundations for a new science of learning. *Science, 325,* 284–288. doi:10.1126/science.1175626

Meltzoff, A. N., & Moore, M. K. (1997). Explaining facial imitations: A theoretical model. *Early Development and Parenting, 6,* 179–192. Retrieved from http://web.media.mit.edu/~coryk/old/Papers/RobotReadings/meltzoff_moore.pdf

Miller, D. C., & DeFina, P. A. (2010). The application of neuroscience to the practice of school neuropsychology. In D. C. Miller (Ed.), *Best practices in school neuropsychology* (pp. 141–157). Hoboken, NJ: Wiley.

Moffitt, T. E., Arsenault, L., Belsky, D., Dickson, N., Hancox, R. J., Harrington, H., . . . Caspi, A. (2011). A gradient of childhood self-control predicts health, wealth, and public safety. *Proceedings of the National Academy of Sciences, 108*(7), 2693–2698.

Montanaro, S. Q. (1991). *Understanding the human being: The importance of the first three years of life*. Mountain View, CA: Nienhaus Montessori.

Montagu, A. (1986). *Touching: The human significance of skin* (3rd ed.). New York, NY: Morrow.

Montessori, M. (1967). *The absorbent mind*. New York, NY: Holt, Rinehart and Winston.

Mueller, C. M., & Dweck, C. S. (1998). Praise for intelligence can undermine children's motivation and performance. *Journal for Personality and Social Psychology, 75*(1), 33–52.

Murray, B., & Fortinberry, A. (2006). *Raising an optimistic child: A proven plan for depression-proofing young children—for life*. New York, NY: McGraw-Hill.

Nakata, T., & Trehub, S. E. (2004). Infants' responsiveness to maternal speech and singing. *Infant Behavior & Development, 27*, 455–464. Retrieved from https://www.utm.utoronto.ca/infant-child-centre/sites/files/infant-child-centre/public/shared/sandra-trehub/003.pdf

The National Campaign to Prevent Teen and Unplanned Pregnancy. (2011, June 9). Teen childbearing cost taxpayers $10.9 billion in 2008 [Press release]. Retrieved from http://www.thenationalcampaign.org/costs/pdf/counting-it-up/press-release-national.pdf

National Organization on Fetal Alcohol Syndrome. (2012). Key facts on alcohol and pregnancy. Retrieved from http://www.nofas.org/factsheets

National Organization on Fetal Alcohol Syndrome–South Dakota (NOFAS-SD). (2009). *Fetal alcohol spectrum disorders education strategies: Working with students with a fetal alcohol spectrum disorder in the education system*. Retrieved from the Center for Disabilities, Sanford School of Medicine, University of South Dakota: http://www.usd.edu/medical-school/center-for-disabilities/upload/fasdeducationalstrategies.pdf

National Scientific Council on the Developing Child. (2005). *Excessive stress disrupts the architecture of the developing brain: Working paper 3*. Retrieved from the Center on the Developing Child, Harvard University: http://developingchild.harvard.edu/index.php/resources/reports_and_working_papers/working_papers/wp3

Neve, C. D., Hart, L., & Thomas, E. (1986, October). Huge learning jumps show potency of brain-based instruction. *Phi Delta Kappan, 68*(2), 143–148.

Newman, J. D., & Harris, J. C. (2009, January). The scientific contributions of Paul D. MacLean (1913–2007). *The Journal of Nervous and Mental Disease, 197*(1), 3–5. Retrieved from http://udn.nichd.nih.gov/pdf/MacLean%20tribute.pdf

NICHD Early Child Care Research Network. (2005). Pathways to reading: The role of oral language in the transition to reading. *Developmental Psychology, 41*(2), 428–442. doi:10.1037/0012-1649.41.2.428

Pellegrino, J. W., & Hilton, M. L. (2012). *Education for life and work: Developing transferable knowledge and skills in the 21st century*. Washington, DC: National Academies Press.

Perlmutter, D., & Colman, C. (2006). *Raise a smarter child by kindergarten: Build a better brain and increase IQ up to 30 points*. New York, NY: Morgan Road Books.

Perry, B., & Szalavitz, M. (2007). *The boy who was raised as a dog and other stories from a child psychiatrist's notebook: What traumatized children can teach us about loss, love, and healing*. New York, NY: Basic Books.

Piaget, J. (1977). *The grasp of consciousness.* London, UK: Routledge.

Ramey, C. T., & Ramey, S. L. (1999). *Right from birth: Building your child's foundation for life.* New York, NY: Goddard Press.

Rampell, C. (2009, August 27). SAT scores and family income. The New York Times Economix blog. Retrieved from http://economix.blogs.nytimes.com/2009/08/27/sat-scores-and-family-income

Rauscher, F. H., Shaw, G. D., Levine, L. J., Wright, E. L., Dennis, W. R., & Newcomb, R. L. (1997). Music training causes long-term enhancement of preschool children's spatial-temporal reasoning. *Neurological Research, 19,* 2–8. Retrieved from http://faculty.washington.edu/demorest/rauscher.pdf

Restak, R. (2009). *Think smart: A neuroscientist's prescription for improving your brain's performance.* New York, NY: Riverhead.

Rodriguez-Gil, G. (2004). The sense of smell: A powerful sense. *reSources, 11*(2). Retrieved from http://www.tsbvi.edu/seehear/summer05/smell.htm

Roskos, K. A., Christie, J. F., & Richgels, D. (2003). *The essentials of early literacy instruction.* Washington, DC: National Association for the Education of Young Children. Retrieved from http://www.naeyc.org/files/yc/file/200303/Essentials.pdf

Rushton, S., Juola-Rushton, A., & Larkin, E. (2010). Neuroscience, play, and early childhood education: Connections, implications, and assessment. *Early Childhood Education Journal, 37,* 351–361. doi:10.1007/s10643-009-0359-3

Safe Kids USA. (2008). *Report to the nation: Trends in unintentional childhood injury mortality and parental views on child safety.* Retrieved from http://www.safekids.org/assets/docs/ourwork/research/research-report-safe-kids-week-2008.pdf

Schaefer, S., Gates, S., & Kiernan, M. (2010). *Strengthening New York businesses through investments in early care and education: A report by America's Edge.* Retrieved from http://www.ocfs.state.ny.us/main/reports/Create_Jobs_Through_Early_Education.pdf

Scheffler, I. (2010). *Of human potential: An essay in the philosophy of education.* New York, NY: Routledge.

Seligman, M. E. P., Reivich, K., Jaycox, L., & Gillham, J. (2007). *The optimistic child: A proven program to safeguard children against depression and build lifelong resilience.* Boston, MA: Houghton Mifflin.

Seligman, M. E. P. (2011). *Flourish: A visionary new understanding of happiness and well-being.* New York, NY: Free Press.

Shenouda, N., Gabel, L., & Timmons, B. W. (2011, July). Physical activity and motor skill development. *Preschooler Focus.* Retrieved from http://www.canchild.ca/en/childrenfamilies/resources/physical_activity_motor_skill_newsletter_july_2011.pdf

Shoda, Y., Mischel, W., & Peake, P. K. (1990). Predicting adolescent cognitive and self-regulatory competencies from preschool delay of gratification: Identifying diagnostic conditions. *Developmental Psychology, 26*(6), 978–986.

Shonkoff, J. P., Garner, A. S., The Committee on Psychosocial Aspects of Child and Family Health, Committee on Early Childhood, Adoption, and Dependent Care, & Section on Developmental and Behavioral Pediatrics et al. (2012). The lifelong effects of early childhood adversity and toxic stress. *Pediatrics, 129*(1), e232–e246. Retrieved from http://pediatrics.aappublications.org/content/129/1/e232.full.pdf+html?sid=500141e5-b360-4b02-a726-d13f30262553

Shonkoff, J. P., & Phillips, D. A. (Eds.). (2000). *From neurons to neighborhoods: The science of early childhood development.* Washington, DC: National Academy Press.

Sibley, B. A., & Etnier, J. L. (2003). The relationship between physical activity and cognition in children: A meta-analysis. *Pediatric Exercise Science, 14,* 243–256. Retrieved from http://peandhealth.wikispaces.com/file/view/Sibley+and+Etnier+2003.pdf

Stamm, J. (2007). *Bright from the start.* New York, NY: Gotham Books.

Stanovich, K. E. (1986). Matthew effects in reading: Some consequences of individual differences in the acquisition of literacy. *Reading Research Quarterly, 21,* 360–407.

Stewart, G. (2005). *Fetal alcohol syndrome.* Detroit, MI: Thompson Gale.

Storch, S. A., & Whitehurst, G. J. (2001). The role of family and home in the literacy development of children from low-income backgrounds. *New Directions for Child and Adolescent Development, 2001*(92), 53–72. doi:10.1002/cd.15.

Storch, S. A., & Whitehurst, G. J. (2002). Oral language and code-related precursors to reading: Evidence from a longitudinal structural model. *Developmental Psychology, 38*(6), 934–947.

Strickland, D. S., & Shanahan, T. (2004). Laying the groundwork for literacy. *Educational Leadership, 61*(6), 74–77.

Strickland, D. S., Morrow, M., Neuman, S. C., Roskos, K., Schickedanz, J. A., & Vukelich, C. (2004). The role of literacy in early childhood. *The Reading Teacher, 58*(1), 86–100.

Sylwester, R. (1995). *A celebration of neurons: An educator's guide to the human brain.* Alexandria, VA: Association for Supervision and Curriculum Development.

Sylwester, R. (2005). *How to explain a brain: An educator's handbook of brain terms and cognitive processes.* Thousand Oaks, CA: Corwin Press.

Sylwester, R. (2010). *A child's brain: The need for nurture.* Thousand Oaks, CA: Corwin Press.

Tayler, C. (2013). Entry to school. In J. Hattie & E. M. Anderman (Eds.), *International guide to student achievement* (pp. 25–27). New York, NY: Routledge.

Teen Parent Child Care Quality Improvement Project. (2005). *Social support: Improving outcomes for adolescent parents and their children.* Tallahassee, FL: Florida State University Center for Prevention and Early Intervention Policy. Retrieved from http://www.cpeip.fsu.edu/resourceFiles/resourceFile_77.pdf

Thomas, A., & Chess, S. (1977). *Temperament and development.* New York, NY: Brunner/Mazel.

Timmons, B. W., Proudfoot, N. A., MacDonald, M. J., Bray, S. R., & Cairney, J. (2012). The health outcomes and physical activity in preschoolers (HOPP) study: Rationale and design. *BMC Public Health, 12.* doi:10.1186/1471-2458-12-284

Torpy, J. M., Lynm, C., & Glass, R. M. (2008). Genetics: The basics. *JAMA, 299*(11), 1388. doi:10.1001/jama.299.11.1388

Torrance, N., & Olson, D. R. (2009). *The Cambridge handbook of literacy.* Cambridge, England: Cambridge University Press.

Tough, P. (2012). *How children succeed: Grit, curiosity, and the hidden power of character.* New York, NY: Houghton Mifflin Harcourt.

Tracy, A. E., & Maroney, D. I. (1999). *Your premature baby and child: Helpful answers and advice for parents.* New York, NY: Berkeley.

United Nations Department of Economic and Social Affairs, Population Division. (2011). *World population prospects: The 2010 revision* [CD-ROM]. New York, NY: United Nations.

U.S. Census Bureau. (2010). *Statistical abstract of the United States: 2010* (129th ed.). Washington, DC: Government Printing Office.

U.S. Department of Agriculture (2011, August 15). USDA announces historic school nutrition improvements as children return to school [Press release]. Retrieved from http://www.fns.usda.gov/pressrelease/2011/035911

U.S. Department of Agriculture. (2012). *Food groups.* Retrieved from http://www.choosemyplate.gov/food-groups

U.S. Deptartment of Agriculture Center for Nutrition Policy and Promotion. (2011). *Kid-friendly veggies and fruits: 10 tips for making healthy foods more fun for children.* 10 Tips Nutritional Education Series. Retrieved from http://www.choosemyplate.gov/food-groups/downloads/TenTips/DGTipsheet11KidFriendlyVeggiesAndFruits.pdf

U.S. Department of Agriculture, Food and Nutrition Service. (2012a). Healthier US School Challenge Application Kit. Retrieved from http://www.fns.usda.gov/tn/HealthierUS/HUSSCkit_sampleletter.pdf

U.S. Department of Agriculture, Food and Nutrition Service. (2012b). National School Lunch Program fact sheet. Retrieved from http://www.fns.usda.gov/cnd/lunch/aboutlunch/nslpfactsheet.pdf

U.S. Department of Agriculture, Food and Nutrition Service. (2012c). *Reaching those in need: State Supplemental Nutrition Assistance Program participation rates in 2010.* Retrieved from http://www.fns.usda.gov/ora/menu/Published/snap/FILES/Participation/Reaching2010.pdf

U.S. Department of Agriculture, Food and Nutrition Service. (2012d). *WIC program: Total participation.* Retrieved from http://www.fns.usda.gov/pd/26wifypart.htm

U.S. Department of Health and Human Services. (2012). *Child maltreatment 2011.* Retrieved from http://www.acf.hhs.gov/sites/default/files/cb/cm11.pdf

Van Mier, H., Tempel, L. W., Perlmutter, J. S., Raichle, M. E., & Petersen, S. E. (1998). Changes in brain activity during motor learning measured with PET: Effects of hand of performance and practice. *Journal of Neurophysiology, 80,* 2177–2200.

Vygotsky, L. (1978). *Mind in society.* Cambridge, MA: Harvard University Press.

Vygotsky, L., with Kozulin, A. (Ed.). (1986). *Thought and language* (Rev. ed.). Cambridge, MA: MIT Press.

Wang, S., & Ellis, N. (2005). *Evaluating the BrainSMART/Health Wise/Health School Team Program at Brookshire Elementary School: An analysis of BMI trend data from 2001 to 2004.* Winter Park, FL: Winter Park Health Foundation.

Watson, D. C. (2010). *Healthy kids make better students* [PowerPoint presentation]. Winter Park, FL: Winter Park Health Foundation.

Wilson, D. L., & Conyers, M. A. (2009). *Wiring the brain to read: Beginning reading preK–grade 3.* Orlando, FL: BrainSMART.

Wilson, D. L., & Conyers, M. A. (2010). *Courageous learners: Increasing student achievement in diverse learning communities* (3rd ed.). Orlando, FL: BrainSMART.

Wilson, D. L., & Conyers, M. A. (2011a). *BrainSMART 60 strategies for increasing student learning* (4th ed.). Orlando, FL: BrainSMART.

Wilson, D. L., & Conyers, M. A. (2011b). *Thinking for results: Strategies for increasing student achievement by as much as 30 percent* (4th ed.). Orlando, FL: BrainSMART.

Wilson, D. L., & Conyers, M. A. (2013). *Five big ideas for effective teaching: Connecting mind, brain, and education research to classroom practice.* New York, NY: Teachers College Press.

Wilson, D. L., Heverly, L., & Conyers, M. (2011). *BrainSMART early start: Building the brain power of young children* (2nd ed.). Orlando, FL: BrainSMART.

Wolfe, P. (2010). *Brain matters: Translating research into classroom practice* (2nd ed.). Alexandria, VA: Association for Supervision and Curriculum Development.

Wolff, P. (1987). *The development of behavioral states and the expression of emotions in early infancy: New proposals for investigation.* Chicago, IL: University of Chicago Press.

Woolfolk, A. (2010). *Educational psychology* (11th ed.). Upper Saddle River, NJ: Pearson.

World Health Organization. (2010). Millennium development goals: Progress towards the health-related millennium development goals (Fact Sheet no. 29). Retrieved from http://www.who.int/mediacentre/factsheets/fs290/en/index.html

Wright, V. R., Chau, M., & Aratani, Y. (2010). *Who are America's poor children? The official story.* New York, NY: National Center for Children in Poverty, Mailman School of Public Health, Columbia University. Retrieved from http://www.nccp.org/publications/pdf/text_912.pdf

Zimmer, C. (2011, Spring). Doublethink: The slight differences between the hemispheres may soup up the brain's processing power. *Discover Magazine Presents the Brain,* 69–70.

Index

About the Authors

Donna Wilson, PhD, is an educational and school psychologist whose work in cognitive education focuses on cognition in the classroom, metacognition, attention, memory, motivation, and approaches and strategies to improve teaching and learning for students of all ages. Donna is an adjunct professor and lead developer of graduate programs with a major in Brain-Based Teaching with the Abraham S. Fischler School of Education at Nova Southeastern University and head of academic affairs for the Center for Innovative Education and Prevention. Her passion is for empowering educators with the resources they need to help all learners reach more of their unique potential.

Marcus Conyers is an author and international speaker on innovating, learning, leading, and developing 21st-century competencies. His global perspective has been honed by his work in 30 countries and in statewide initiatives with the Florida Department of Education. He has led a National Association of Elementary School Principals summer conference and was keynote speaker for a conference of the South African Principals' Association. Marcus serves as director of communications for the Center for Innovative Education and Prevention, a not-for-profit organization with the mission of "empowering potential across the life span." He is passionate about ensuring that all children experience opportunities to flourish in the first five years and beyond.